THE DERBY YEARBOOK

The Derby Yearbook

Celebrating 40 Years of City Status

Written by the People of Derby

EDITED BY CONNOR BROWN

peregrine

peregrine

Peregrine Publishing aims to publish a broad range of fiction
and non-fiction titles that will appeal locally, regionally and
nationally. Based within the Department of Humanities at
the University of Derby, it is partly run and administered
by postgraduate and undergraduate Publishing students.

The Derby Yearbook is Peregrine's first publication.

The Derby Yearbook: Celebrating 40 Years of City Status

First edition, 2017

Text copyright © contributors

Published by Peregrine Publishing
University of Derby
Kedleston Road, Derby DE22 1GB
www.peregrinepublishing.co.uk

ISBN 978-1-912312-00-9

Cover design by Luke Taplin-McCallum
Cover images: © Alison Loydall, © Carnegie

Designed and typeset in 10/14 Monotype Pastonchi by Peregrine Publishing
Printed and bound in the UK by Charlesworth Press, Wakefield

Contents

Foreword

Stoker Devonshire, 12th Duke of Devonshire KCVO CBE DL

THE CITY OF DERBY has always been very important to my family, ever since the time of Bess of Hardwick, the matriarch of the Cavendish dynasties. Her magnificent tomb in the nave of what is now Derby Cathedral (see page 52) is a constant reminder to me of my family's long and deep relationship with the City of Derby, echoing a similar relationship with the county.

Since my wife and I arrived to live and work at Chatsworth at the beginning of 2006 we have come to know the city a great deal better than hitherto. My involvement with the University of Derby, as Chancellor, and my term of office as a Trustee of Derby Museums Trust – of which I am now the Patron – have meant many visits to the city, and thus our discovery of so much of interest and the opportunity to make new friendships with people of the city.

Peregrine 'Stoker' Cavendish, 12th Duke of Devonshire, outside the family home, Chatsworth. This stately home in the Derbyshire Dales stands on the east bank of the river Derwent and has been home to the Cavendish family since 1549.
SOURCE: CHATSWORTH

The University of Derby has been an extraordinary triumph. In just 25 years it has grown and improved beyond the most optimistic ambitions of those dedicated people who achieved its inauguration, an event which was considered by most to be virtually impossible (pages 66–73).

The Derby Museums Trust has also been a success; having become its own Trust in 2012 and thus separated from the direct control of the City Council (but still receiving the vast majority of its funding from that authority) it has blossomed into a vibrant and energetic museum. Pickford's House (see pages 49–50) and the museum itself (see pages 37–44) are thriving, and most exciting of all is the current re-modelling of the Silk Mill (see pages 45–8) for what will soon be the Museum of Making. What more appropriate cultural offering could there be for the City of Derby, steeped as it is in invention, design, manufacturing, and innovative thinking. 'Making' is what has made the city great, what makes it great today, and what will make it greater yet tomorrow.

I mention the university and the Museums Trust as parts of Derby that I am excited about and proud of because I am intimate with them both. But, reading this book, there is so much more to impress, so many facets of life in this wonderful place, in this amazing city.

How timely that this book is being published and how exciting it is to know that it will introduce many thousands of people from all over the world to the glories of Derby, its institutions, its businesses, its history, its culture, its buildings, and, most importantly of all, its people: a wonderfully diverse and eclectic population which will drive the city forward to new successes and international acclaim.

My congratulations to those who have enabled this book to be written and published, they do the City of Derby a great and well-deserved service.

Chatsworth, April 2017

Preface

Connor Brown, Editor

T HE IDEA of this book was born of the desire to commemorate Derby's first forty years of city status, but the town's history stretches far further than that (see pages 1–12). *The Derby Yearbook* is concerned with those companies, institutions, and people that have had a significant impact on the life, culture, and economy of modern Derby, a city that gained its status as such in 1977 (see pages 13–14). The book gives Derbeians and those with an affinity for the city an opportunity to present personal accounts of its modern-day activities and historical foundations.

The Derby Yearbook takes readers on a tour through Derby's famed industrial heritage, varied religious make-up, leading educational institutions, pioneering festivals and art collectives, decorated sports teams, and bustling commerce of past and present. A book of so few pages could never aspire nor claim to capture all that Derby has to offer. It does modestly hope, however, to provide a snapshot of the city on its fortieth anniversary.

This book was a truly collective effort, pooling the knowledge of 40 authors and a small army of other helpers – an army almost outnumbering that of Bonnie Prince Charlie (see pages 15–17). These people get a fuller mention in the acknowledge-ments, but deserve much more than two references in a book that could not have been made without them. The community spirit contained within this book, and that shown by those involved in its creation, is testament to the spirit of Derby: a proud city that has much to say and so much to offer others.

Derby, May 2017

The earliest known map of Derby, by John Speed, 1610. At this time Derby was a county town notable, according to William Camden, for 'its retail trade [in] ... corn'. The population was tiny, perhaps 3,000 at this time, but the town played an important economic, administrative and social role within the county of Derbyshire and the low-lying agricultural region around the Derwent and the Trent. John Speed is England's most famous Stuart cartographer. He hand-drew this map, titled *Anno Darbieshire Described*.

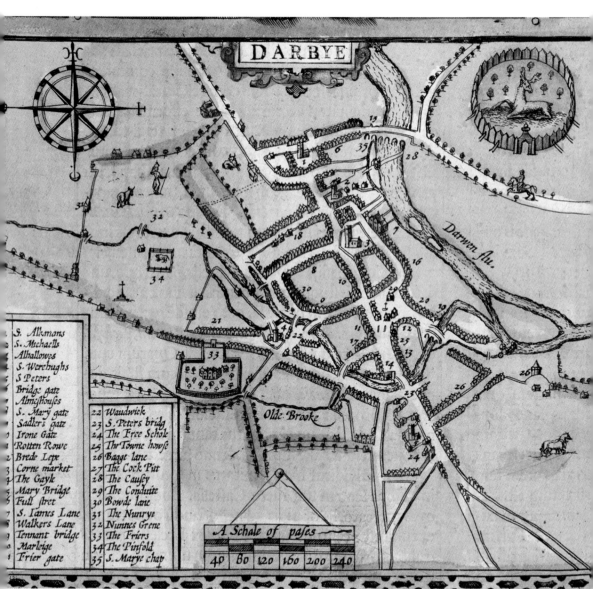

DARBYE

S. Alkmans	22	Waudwick
S. Michaells	23	S. Peters bridg
Alhallowes	24	The Free Schole
S. Werebughs	25	The Towne howse
S Peters	26	Bagge lane
Bridge gate	27	The Cock Pit
Almeshouses	28	The Caufy
S. Mary gate	29	The Conduite
Sadlers gate	30	Bowde lane
Irone Gate	31	The Nunrye
Rotten Rowe	32	Nunnes Grene
Brede Lepe	33	The Friers
Corne market	34	The Pinfold
The Gayle	35	S. Marye chap
Mary Bridge		
Full ftret		
S. Iames Lane		
Walkers Lane		
Tennant bridge		
Marleige		
Frier gate		

Darwen flu.

Olde Brooke

A Schale of pases
40 80 120 160 200 240

'A fine ... and pleasant town'

IN A PROCESS that began around 300 years ago the economy and society – and the towns and cities – of Britain were transformed by the arrival of industry and all that this entailed. The experience of Derby was notable in many ways during this period, as we shall see, but hardly unique. In many ways it is instructive to think of the eighteenth century as the time when the very nature and character of many towns, including Derby, were transformed. Think of this time as a watershed, a period of gradual but sometimes dramatic change. Before 1700 Derby had an important county and regional role, but in most ways was a fairly typical market, trading and 'thoroughfare' town. In the century and a half following that date Derby became something quite different, its economy, transport links and its townscape largely unrecognisable save for a few of the key landmarks. In the period covered by this book Derby has undergone a variety of changes, many of which are documented here.

Despite all the changes – enormous population growth since 1700, the arrival of industry, the railways and now the dual carriageways that carve their unforgiving paths hard by the historic centre – Derby retains some of the ancient features and many of the characteristics that were noted by Daniel Defoe (1720s), William Camden (1610) and others. In Britain one is never far from tangible features of the past, and glimpses of Derby's ancient history can still be seen, including the layout of the town and its streets, or the remnants of Darley Abbey, or St Mary's Bridge Chapel, or even the fact that parts of the A38 to Burton, a structure we regard as so completely modern, actually lies on foundations that were part of the Roman road built almost 2,000 years ago.

One of the abiding features of Derby is its principal river, the Derwent. A thousand years ago the river was providing water and, perhaps more importantly, a source of power, with no fewer than ten corn mills being counted on the Derwent and Markeaton Brook at Derby in 1086. This is a consistent theme through much of Derby history, for only in recent decades has the river *not* been used to power machinery of various sorts. Indeed, the river is probably why Derby is located here at all. The name (originally Northworthy) is Viking in origin, and it would appear fairly certain that the town was established at a suitable crossing point. There was an important medieval bridge here (a remarkable little chapel still exists at one end, perched atop the massive stone springings of the ancient bridge arch). Capital of Mercia, administrative centre, market, and the only 'borough' in Derbyshire at the time of the Norman Conquest, Derby always was an important regional centre.

In some ways the town's perspective lay in two directions. One to the north-west and Derbyshire: described by Edward Browne as 'a strange, mountainous, misty, moorish, rocky, wild country' and by Daniel Defoe as 'a waste and howling wilderness'. Derby was the county town, Derbyshire's largest and most important urban centre. The other perspective was to the fertile, low-lying valleys of the Derwent and Trent valleys. This was important to the young town, not only because of the agricultural riches with which the district was endowed (it was noted for 'excellent cheese' among other things), but because the valleys allowed an easy, logical route north for travellers and traders alike.

Pre-industrial Derby, therefore, looked both ways and became a significant trading town. For centuries lead had been mined in the area around Wirksworth (in Derby Museum you can still see a 65 kg bar of lead from Roman times that had been mined there and which turned up in Yeaveley 1,800 years later), and Derby acted as a market for this commodity and many others, including corn, wool, wood, food, malt and other produce, some of it traded on little ships that could make it up the river as far as the Derby bridge in the Middle Ages.

A Bronze Age boat known as the Hanson Log Boat. It was discovered resting in a gravel pit in Shardlow village, Derbyshire, in 1998. The boat was almost complete but was slightly damaged by quarry machinery before its importance had been identified. Following its £119,000 conservation, it is now on display in Derby Museum.

SOURCE: © CARNEGIE, WITH PERMISSION OF DERBY MUSEUM AND ART GALLERY

To His Grace the   Duke of Devonshire,
THIS VIEW OF DERBY   FROM THE MEADOWS,
Is with Permission most respectfully Dedicated   by his Grace's obliged & obedient humble Servant,   Henry Burn

Derby from the Meadows, 1846. Henry Burn's view looks up the river Derwent, where you can see the tower of the church of All Saints (from 1927 Derby Cathedral) in the distance.

SOURCE: © CARNEGIE, WITH PERMISSION OF DERBY MUSEUM AND ART GALLERY

Its status as a 'thoroughfare' town meant that travellers, or 'foreigners' as they were sometimes called, were a common sight on Derby's streets, and in its many inns and guest houses. In the late seventeenth century Derby, itself with a population of perhaps only 4,000, had no fewer than 841 bed spaces for travellers and 547 stable places for their horses. One-third of Derbyshire's guest beds could be found in Derby. People from afar came here on business or just passing through, just as they do today, where many of the city's hotel and guest rooms are taken up on short-term lets by business or industry people involved in one of the many large manufacturing concerns that are a remarkable feature of the district's economy in the twenty-first century. Some themes in Derby's history are remarkably persistent and resilient.

From early times, too, Derby could boast some 'industry', or 'busy-ness' as it was sometimes quaintly known. There were maltsters and brewers; pottery making from at least the twelfth century; according to Celia Fiennes there were many glove-makers in the town; as early as the fifteenth century the town and district was known for making scythes; there was a small iron industry, smelting ironstone that developed in time into a major heavy industry here; and the town was well known for its artisan craftsmen, its merchants, its traders, and its carriers. It was a small but busy place long before the arrival of what we would now recognise as modern industry.

A gentle breeze of change began to lift around the end of the seventeenth century, a time of innovation and new technology. Later times would bring larger and more profound changes, but, as we have seen, the cusp of the eighteenth century, around 1700, stands as a hugely significant period in Derby's history. Several people typify this, including George Sorocold, an inspired engineer from Lancashire. In 1692, he designed and installed a new pumped water supply for the town centre, with a waterwheel and four miles of elm pipes. He rehung the bells of All Saints, but is perhaps best known for helping with the construction of both of Derby's

Derby, 1806. Little signs of industry are everywhere: the Silk Mill (the 'Italian' Works and the Doubling Shed), a China Works across the river, an 'ornament manufactory', and Evans' slitting and rolling mills powered by the river.

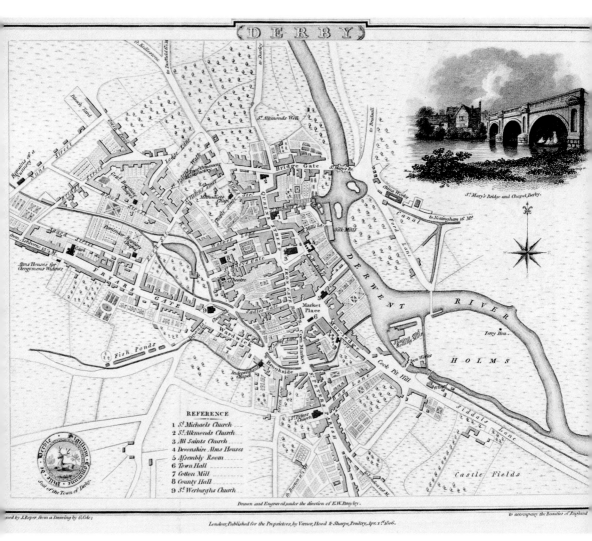

Rowe. Cheltenham   DERBY RAILWAY STATION & MIDLAND HOTEL   _Published by W. Adam Matlo..._

Lithograph by George
Rowe (1796–1864) showing
views of the North
Midland Railway station
building (*left*) and the
Midland Hotel. Formed
in the 1830s, the North
Midland Railway ran
from Derby to Leeds.
In 1844 this railway
combined with the York
& North Midland,
Midland Counties, and
the Birmingham &
Derby Railways to form
the Midland Railway.
The Grade II listed
Midland Hotel was
designed by Francis
Thompson for the
Midland Railway in 1842.

SOURCE: SCIENCE & SOCIETY
PICTURE LIBRARY © SCIENCE
MUSEUM

first textile mills: Cotchett's silk mill of 1704 and the world-famous Lombes' mill adjacent to it in the 1720s.

These innovative structures used the water flow of the Derwent for power. Derby's new mills were built on a small island in the river, involving large engineering works and money. In Derby inward investment for industrial development was an important phenomenon from an early date.

As we shall see (pages 45–8) Derby's Silk Mill was significant as one of the very earliest true 'factories' in the country, if not the world. And it is significant that it was involved in textile manufacture, in this case the spinning (or 'throwing' as it was known) of silk thread. Textiles, almost everywhere, was the first sector to industrialise, and it did so earliest – or, rather, most spectacularly – here in Britain. The Silk Mill did well, but apart from a few similar mills in Macclesfield and Manchester it was not until later in the century that large-scale change came to the Derwent Valley.

By this time, the 1770s onwards, cotton had become the most important material in Derbyshire and Lancashire, and innovators such as the Arkwrights, at Cromford and elsewhere, and the Strutts at Belper, built enormous cotton spinning mills whose machinery was driven by waterwheels driven by the reliable flow of the Derwent. Economic migrants came in search of work, and in order to attract young families the mill entrepreneurs built houses, sponsored other industries (in the case of Belper, nail making) and created new communities which all looked in part to Derby as their retail and market centre. Industry had arrived in Derby, and unlike many other places, it has never left.

'A FINE ... AND PLEASANT TOWN'   5

Textiles led the way: not only silk, and cotton, but hosiery, as elsewhere in the region to the south and east. In 1789, when revolution was gripping Bourbon France, 170 Derby framework knitters were beavering away, and 1,156 frames were enumerated. Pottery, too, with George III, no less, lending the name 'Royal' to the Crown Derby works in 1773.

The town grew and prospered. It became a regional centre for the intellectual ferment known as the Enlightenment, with figures such as Erasmus Darwin, and organisations such as the Lunar Society and the Derby Philosophical Society prominent in the region. High art, too, in the remarkable paintings of Joseph Wright as well as the astonishing ironwork of Robert Bakewell that can be seen most easily in the rebuilt, eighteenth-century church of All Saints (founded c.943; rebuilt 1723; and since 1927 Derby Cathedral), at Melbourne Hall, and outside the Silk Mill, where his elaborate gates survive.

Iron working was to become another important local employer, with some 1,200 at least employed at the height of the Victorian era, making castings for bridges (such as the famous one over Friargate) and many other iron products. Heavy industry had come to Derby in the form of Evans' water-powered slitting and rolling mill on the river, and by the time Victoria had came to the throne the town had several

Lithograph of the interior of the North Midland Railway station by G. Russel, 1839.

DERBY STATION — NORTH MIDLAND RAILWAY.
FRANCIS THOMPSON, ARCH.

Midland Counties
RAILWAY.

THE PUBLIC ARE INFORMED, THAT THIS RAILWAY,

FROM

Nottingham and Derby,

TO

LOUGHBORO', LEICESTER,

AND THE INTERMEDIATE STATIONS,

Will be opened for the conveyance of Passengers, Parcels, Gentlemen's Carriages, Horses, and Van Goods, on TUESDAY the 5th of May.

HOURS OF DEPARTURE.

From Nottingham and Derby to Leicester.	From Leicester to Nottingham and Derby.
Eight o'Clock Morning	* * * Half past Seven Morning
Half past Eleven Morning	* * Eleven o'Clock Morning
Quarter to Five Afternoon	* Three o'Clock Afternoon
Quarter to Eight Evening	Half past Seven Evening
ON SUNDAYS.	ON SUNDAYS.
Eight o'Clock Morning	Half past Seven Morning
Half past Seven Evening.	Seven o'Clock Evening.

On the opening of the North Midland Railway, the Eight o'Clock Morning, and Quarter to Five o'Clock Afternoon Trains from Derby to Leicester, will be in connection with the Trains leaving Sheffield for Derby at Half past Five Morning, and Two o'Clock Afternoon.
The Half past Seven and Eleven o'Clock Morning Trains from Leicester, will arrive in Derby in time for the Nine o'Clock Morning and Quarter to One o'Clock Afternoon Trains from Derby to Sheffield.
The Train marked * * * is in connection at Derby with Coaches to Ashbourne, Leek, Macclesfield, Stockport, Manchester, and Liverpool; also to Matlock, Bakewell, and Buxton ; and at Nottingham, with Coaches to Mansfield, Newark, Lincoln, Hull, &c.
The Train marked * * is in connection at Nottingham with a Coach to Southwell, Retford, and Gainsborough.
The Train marked * is in connection at Nottingham with Coaches to Mansfield, Southwell, Newark, and Lincoln.

THE INTERMEDIATE STATIONS ARE
KEGWORTH, BARROW, SILEBY, AND SYSTON.

It is requested that Passengers will be at the intermediate Stations, and Carriages and Horses at principal Stations, a quarter of an Hour *before* the time advertised for starting.
The Doors of the Booking Offices at principal Stations will be closed precisely at the Hours appointed for departure; after which no one can be admitted to go by the Train.

FARES.

	FIRST CLASS.	SECOND CLASS.
From Nottingham to Leicester	6s. 0d.	4s. 6d.
From Derby to Leicester	6s. 0d.	5s. 0d.
From Nottingham to Loughborough	3s. 6d.	2s. 6d.
From Derby to Loughborough	3s. 6d.	3s. 0d.
From Leicester to Loughborough	2s. 6d.	2s. 0d.

RATES FOR PARCELS AND VAN GOODS.

Of and under 18lbs weight, for any distance under 30 Miles	6d.
Above 18lbs. and under 28lbs	9d.
Above 28lbs. and under 56lbs.	1s. 0d.
Above 56lbs. and under 112lbs.	1s. 6d.
Above 112lbs. 1s. 6d. per Cwt.	

N.B.—The above Rates include delivery and all other charges, except the customary Two-pence for Booking.
Persons desirous of having their Parcels, &c. by Railway, are requested to mark them conspicuously " Per Railway."
The Company will not be responsible for Parcels, &c. above the value of £10. unless declared as such at the time of booking, and entered and paid for accordingly.
In addition to the Offices at the Railway Stations, the following Receiving Houses have been appointed : where information relative to the Trains may be obtained :—In NOTTINGHAM, White Lion and May-pole.—DERBY, the Bell, King's Head, Tiger, and New Inn.—LOUGHBOROUGH, Red Lion.—LEICESTER, Stag and Pheasant.

(By order) **J. F. BELL,** *Secretary.*

Nottingham, April 28th, 1840.

J. HICKLIN, PRINTER, PELHAM STREET, NOTTINGHAM.

1924-450

Original poster advertising the opening of the railway, 5 May 1840. Some of the detail is fascinating. When the very first railway of this type, from Liverpool to Manchester, was being conceived in the 1820s it was assumed that freight would be the most important income stream, but it soon became apparent that passenger traffic would be more lucrative than parcels. Here, therefore, we see passenger rates listed before those for freight.

SCIENCE & SOCIETY PICTURE LIBRARY © NATIONAL RAILWAY MUSEUM

significant iron foundries. A wide range of iron products, such as post boxes for the Royal Mail and kitchen ranges, made by companies such as Handysides, would soon be supplemented by railway-related engineering, with one firm, Eastwoods, for example, specialising in railway wheels.

In 1840 the railway opened from Derby. This, along with the establishment of railway engineering in the town (itself influenced and helped by the large number of existing iron works), had a transformative effect on Derby's economy and society. Reports had it that the city fathers of Nottingham felt that the noise and smoke pollution, as well as the inevitable influx of perhaps rowdy passengers, would not be suitable for their town, and so the Midland Railway came to Derby, which quickly became an important hub in what was quickly to become a national network of competing private railways. The railway brought passengers, and trade, but also

Livestock booking office for the Royal Agricultural Show, Derby, June 1906. This is where people wanting to put their livestock onto trains to and from the show booked them in.

SOURCE: SCIENCE & SOCIETY PICTURE LIBRARY © NATIONAL RAILWAY MUSEUM

and perhaps more importantly employment for thousands of Derby people and incomers. In some ways the growth of the railway network mirrored earlier, and indeed later, patterns of transport links, with towns such as Derby continuing to occupy crucial positions and providing important communications links to all compass points.

Victorian Derby was a busy town, where industry flourished and the population grew, partly by in-migration and partly by natural increase. In time the town gained all of the civic features one would expect, from hospitals and schools, to football and cricket teams, theatres, an arboretum, shops, pubs, churches and parks. And as with all similar towns its housing, infrastructure, water supply and sanitation systems struggled to cope with rising population numbers and crowded districts. For a long period in the nineteenth and earlier twentieth centuries housing conditions for working people were often poor, and the town's first serious attempts to improve the housing stock by removing unsuitable older dwellings only really began in the 1890s.

With the new century came continued economic and social development and change. In 1907 a small motor car company by the name of Rolls-Royce was attracted to Derby by the promise of being able to pay lower wages than in Manchester. War then led to engineering work on aircraft, and while car manufacturing moved to Crewe, the aero work continued, and continues, to thrive here.

Indeed, engineering and economic investment are consistent themes in Derby's history, and the city and district now provide what is, for the UK, a remarkably high proportion of skilled manufacturing and engineering jobs, at large plants such as Bombardier, Rolls-Royce, JCB and Toyota.

Buffet refreshment trolley
with attendant, Derby
station, 23 February 1908.
Refreshments on offer
include fruit, Bovril,
hot milk and Bollinger
champagne. Nowadays
the on-board trolley is
more likely to include
crisps, chocolate, and
cans of lager. How times
change.

SCIENCE & SOCIETY PICTURE
LIBRARY © NATIONAL
RAILWAY MUSEUM

Mirroring social change across the country, too, Derby's population is still growing and contains a higher proportion of black and minority ethnic communities than at any time in the past: 24.7 per cent in 2011.

What themes and common strands can we discern from this long history? The Roman general who decided to build a fort, *Derventio*, to the east of the Derwent two millennia ago made a sensible choice, for Derby's central and nodal location has always been important. Derby remains important to the county, though it has lost administrative responsibility to Matlock. The city also remains vitally important to the economy of its region, and now also has an economic importance far beyond its region, with highly advanced manufactured goods, and services, being traded and sold around the globe from locations with DE postcodes. Culturally, too, the spirit of the Enlightenment lives on, with theatres, festivals and events of wide variety and appeal.

Every town has a character that has been shaped by its particular history, and by the collective experience of the people who live and work there. As the pages of this book show, today's residents of Derby have every right to be proud of their city.

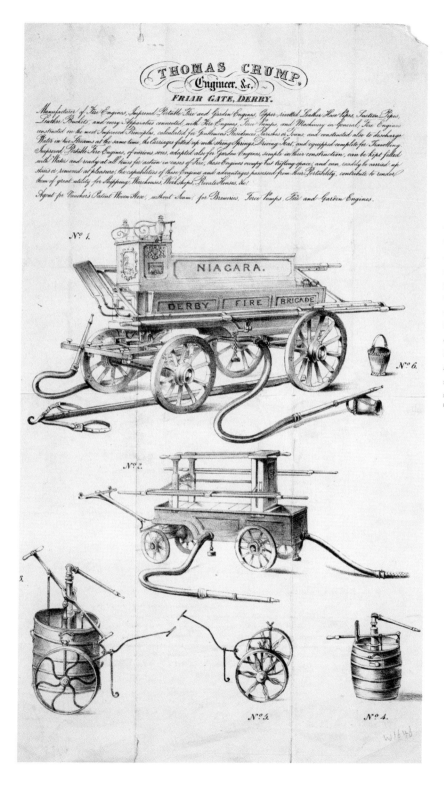

ABOVE

Such was the importance of the railway industry to Derby, and so high were the war casualties among its workers that the Midland Railway commissioned its own war memorial, here seen being unveiled to commemorate almost 3,000 fallen in the First World War.

SCIENCE & SOCIETY PICTURE LIBRARY © NATIONAL RAILWAY MUSEUM

BELOW

Horse-drawn tram services such as this were introduced in 1880 and ran for only 27 years until this photograph was taken to commemorate the last journey. This is at the corner of Ashbourne Road and Surrey Street, 1907.

SCIENCE & SOCIETY PICTURE LIBRARY © PAST PIX

How Derby Became a City

Robin Wood, former mayor

C ITY STATUS, like all honours under the Royal Prerogative, is granted very sparingly. Derby petitioned unsuccessfully to become a city in 1935, a century after the Municipal Corporations Act. In 1954, 800 years since Derby's first charter, another attempt failed. Derby's borders were vastly expanded in 1968, but a further request was denied by the Home Office. In 1974 Derby lost most of its key functions to an overriding county council in Matlock, and the appetite for civic pride withered to an all-time low.

However, a Conservative opposition councillor for Chaddesden Ward, Gerald Andrews, fought tirelessly to revive a sense of pride in Derby and moved a motion to Derby District Council, not only to apply for borough status (thereby retaining our centuries-old tradition of a mayoralty) but also for Derby to become a city. Some Labour members argued against both: Litchurch councillor, Bob Newton, for example, voted against both proposals, accepting the mayoralty of the city a few years later. The leader of the Labour-controlled council, John Dilks, argued that the cost of changing printed council letter heading would be 'indefensible'.

The motion in favour of borough status was narrowly accepted and successfully bore fruit in letters patent, enabling Derby to keep its mayor. The motion for city status was defeated by the same councillors and was therefore not submitted. Undeterred, Gerald Andrews prepared his own submission and, in pre-internet days, created a huge public petition to support it. However, the Home Office advised him that success was unlikely without his council's backing.

In 1976 political control changed back to the Conservatives with a majority of just one, under the leadership of Darley councillor Ronald Longdon JP, who embraced Gerald Andrews' popular arguments and suggested that the application should be aligned to the forthcoming Silver Jubilee.

In May 1977 the incoming mayor, Jeffery Tillett, the first Conservative to hold that office for four years, said in his acceptance speech that he sincerely hoped that he would be the last elected mayor of the borough, and that city status, 'a pipe dream' of so many of his predecessors, would soon be a reality. Within weeks it was just that.

Her Majesty duly arrived on 28 July 1977, and on the steps of the Council House,

Derby Council House on Derwent and Corporation Street, the home of Derby City Council, was built 1939–41. In 2012 it reopened after a £32 million refurbishment. The exact figure spent on the refurbishment of Derby's other council houses is unknown. Derby City Council has 51 councillors, with three councillors representing each of the 17 wards of the city.

SOURCE: © ALISON LOYDALL

in front of a cheering crowd of thousands of Derby burghers, presented Jeffery Tillett with the letters patent that made them, for the first time, Derby citizens, granting them 'all such rank, liberties, privileges and immunities as are incident to a City'.

And what were these liberties and privileges? Only time has been able to tell. The idea was extremely popular at the time and a cause of much celebration. Derby's first beer festival was inaugurated by the mayor and there were charter celebrations once the new Assembly Rooms were opened at a further royal occasion on 9 November of the same year. Even Derby County Football Club took out an advertisement in the *Evening Telegraph* to state that they would not be changing their name to Derby City Football Club. The same paper's headline writers used the short word 'city' as often as they could, having always hitherto had trouble with 'Derby County Borough Council' and preferring to opt for the inaccurate term, 'Town Council'. A rather surprised Borough Secretary, Borough Engineer, and Borough Treasurer all suddenly found they had shorter, but far grander titles. Mindful of John Dilks' comments, however, the council letter heading was not scrapped, merely overprinted with the word 'City' until stocks were exhausted.

Opinions differ, but as someone involved with most of the above events and the subsequent life of the city, I would argue that events as significant as the arrival of Toyota and the development of Pride Park owe much to our status as a city, which boxes in the same weight class as Nottingham and Leicester; not to mention Sydney, Hong Kong, or New York.

Bonnie Prince Charlie in Derby

Arran Paul Johnston, Director, Scottish Battlefields Trust

O N 4 December 1745 the people of Derby were treated to an extraordinary and unnerving sight: the arrival of an army marching to overthrow King George II. What made the sight all the more curious was that the army was composed mainly of Scottish warriors, including thousands of Highlanders, whose dress, weapons, and language must have appeared totally alien. The finest troops entered Derby first, assembling on horseback in the Market Place. These were the Jacobites, who believed that the exiled James Francis Stuart had a better claim to the throne than George II. They were led by James' charismatic son, Charles Edward Stuart, 'Bonnie Prince Charlie'. The Jacobites' arrival doubled the size of the population, as they lodged in houses around the town, some of which still stand, while the prince resided at the Earl of Exeter's fine house beside the Derwent.

The Jacobites were enjoying an astonishing run of success: they had seized Edinburgh, defeated the redcoats at Prestonpans, and captured Carlisle. They were now just 120 miles from London. But could they succeed in reaching the capital? The

Mannequin of Bonnie Prince Charlie at Derby Museum and Art Gallery. This is a depiction of the scene during the night of Charles Edward Stuart's stay at Exeter House in December 1745 before the retreat of the Jacobite army to Scotland. The room is in fact the very same room, reassembled at the museum.
SOURCE: © ALISON LOYDALL

Re-enactment of Bonnie
Prince Charlie and the
Jacobites on Swarkestone
Bridge, six miles south
of Derby. This was the
farthest point that the
Bonnie Prince and his
6,500 Jacobites reached,
and the last time that
Derbyshire was crossed
by an invading force.
SOURCE: © JOHN WALLS
PHOTOGRAPHY

prince was sure of it, but on 5 December 1745 his senior officers counselled retreat.
They feared the odds were stacking against them and wished instead to return to
Scotland. In bitter meetings at Exeter House they forced Charles to abandon the
march on London; he raged that they were throwing away their only hope of success.
At the old Assembly Rooms the crowd had knocked over the Royal Standard in
their eagerness to see; perhaps this was a bad omen. On the morning of 6 December
1745 the army marched out of Derby down Sadlergate and on to Ashbourne Road. As
the Highlanders realised that they were going backwards, they let out a great groan.
They returned to Scotland where, despite another victory at Falkirk in January, they
were finally defeated at the Battle of Culloden.

The decision at Derby changed the possible course of history, turning the tide of
war irrevocably against the Jacobite cause. There were many among the Derbyshire
gentry who had sympathy with the prince's cause, but there were others like
the Duke of Devonshire who actively raised men to oppose him – the famously
ineffective 'Derby Blues'. These historic events can still be traced on the face of the
city today, from the plaque in the Cathedral where the prince attended a service, to
the Jacobite room in Derby Museum, and the only statue in the world of Charles
Edward Stuart.

Every year on the first weekend of December, Derby's own Charles Edward
Stuart Society brings these events to life to remind us of three days on which Derby
held the fate of kings in its hands. As a young Derbeian I was fascinated by the
city's rich heritage and have since become a professional historian. I have also been
privileged to portray the prince at the city's Jacobite events for many years, and hope
that my doing so helps inspire others as much as living in this city has inspired me.

OPPOSITE
The only public statue
in the world of Charles
Edward Stuart, on
Cathedral Green in
Derby city centre.
SOURCE © CARNEGIE

Erasmus Darwin and the Derby Philosophical Society

Paul Elliott, Professor of Modern History, University of Derby

A SUCCESSFUL PHYSICIAN, Erasmus Darwin (1731–1802) was an influential figure in Derby's history. Darwin moved to Derby in 1783, after leaving Lichfield in 1781 to live at Radburne Hall with his new wife Elizabeth (Pole), taking a townhouse at Full Street near All Saints Church. The Darwin family house had a garden to the rear planted with indigenous and exotic plants, with a specially sunk artesian well and a heated summer house. More land across the Derwent, with an orchard which Darwin called his 'farm', was reached by a wire-led boat.

At Lichfield Darwin had created a thriving midland medical practice and become a founding member of the Lunar Society, an intellectual coterie that included natural philosophers and industrialists such as Josiah Wedgwood (1730–95), James Watt (1736–1819), Matthew Boulton (1728–1809), and John Whitehurst (1713–88). Darwin continued his medical practice at Derby, travelling to see patients in his specially designed carriage or having them stay with his family. He used many conventional Georgian treatments, including bleeding, purgatives, laxatives, blistering, plasters, electricity, and many plant and animal substance-based medicines. He also got to know his patients and their families well, tailoring interventions and recommendations to character and behaviour, such as advocating teetotalism and allowing nature to take its course with the aid of prescribed warm baths, bracing rides, or vigorous walks.

Darwin took a keen interest in national politics and Derby's public affairs: supporting the Derby Society for Political Information created after the French Revolution, treating some poor patients gratis, creating a town dispensary, and campaigning for public health improvements. These included the controversial enclosure of the Nun's Green common lands led by his friend William Strutt (1756–1830), for which, using the full weight of his medical reputation, Darwin contributed to the pamphlet war and attended early meetings of the Improvement Commission with his son Erasmus junior, a Derby attorney.

Darwin's general scientific interests are evident in his voluminous correspondence, mechanical inventions, and publications, including the major books and epic poems published during his final years, as he retired from medical practice. Inspired by

19

a botanic garden created near Lichfield, *The Botanic Garden*, an epic poem with extensive philosophical notes, shot Darwin to literary fame and for a short time

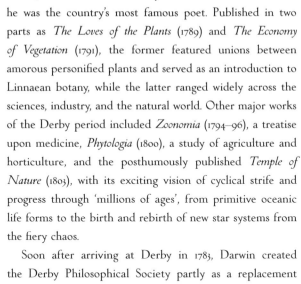

he was the country's most famous poet. Published in two parts as *The Loves of the Plants* (1789) and *The Economy of Vegetation* (1791), the former featured unions between amorous personified plants and served as an introduction to Linnaean botany, while the latter ranged widely across the sciences, industry, and the natural world. Other major works of the Derby period included *Zoonomia* (1794–96), a treatise upon medicine, *Phytologia* (1800), a study of agriculture and horticulture, and the posthumously published *Temple of Nature* (1803), with its exciting vision of cyclical strife and progress through 'millions of ages', from primitive oceanic life forms to the birth and rebirth of new star systems from the fiery chaos.

Soon after arriving at Derby in 1783, Darwin created the Derby Philosophical Society partly as a replacement for regular Lunar Society contacts. The Society brought together professionals, especially medical men, gentry, indus-trialists, and manufacturers. Original members included William Strutt (1756–1830), Revd Thomas Gisborne (1758–1846), Richard French (1739–1801), Dr Peter Crompton (1762–1833), and Brooke Boothby (1744–1824). Although not listed as members, some women did attend meetings, and Georgiana, Duchess of Devonshire (1757–1806), who had interests in mineralogy and electricity, was an honorary member.

Bust of Erasmus Darwin, created by William John Coffee (1774–1846), made from coade stone, c.1795–1815. William John Coffee was an internationally renowned English artist and sculptor who worked predominantly in porcelain, plaster, and terracotta. He spent his early life and career living on Nottingham Road in Derby, but his later life in America.
SOURCE: © 2017 DERBY MUSEUMS TRUST

Darwin emphasised how the Derby Society would be at the vanguard of Enlightenment progress, leading the battle against torpor, ignorance, and anarchy, using the 'daring hand of experimental philosophy' to transcend the 'feeble human frame' and 'enrich the terraqueous globe' with new practical arts, necessities, and 'embellishments of life' to do 'honour to human nature'. The Society formed a library of mainly scientific works and collected editions of the works of other international learned societies. These were circulated among the members, and became an important forum for discussion about the latest developments in the natural sciences, lasting until 1858 when it merged with the Derby Town and County Museum. One offshoot, the Derby Literary and Philosophical Society, created in 1808, introduced programmes of public lectures on scientific and literary subjects and formed a laboratory. The Derbyshire General Infirmary (1809), Derby Mechanics' Institute (1825), and Derby Arboretum (1840) were other institutions partly created by the 'Derby Philosophers'.

John Whitehurst

Jordan Reynolds, Assistant Editor, The Derby Yearbook

JOHN WHITEHURST was born in 1713 in Congleton, Cheshire, to a clockmaker, also named John. He clearly received a good grounding from his father, and went on to become a mechanical genius, a polymath, and an intellectual figure with an astonishingly wide variety of interests and capabilities.

John Whitehurst settled in Derby, but he found it difficult to practise his trade in the town because he was not qualified to do so as a burgess. In order to gain this status, he cannily offered to design and build a 'turret' clock for the tower of the Richard Jackson-designed Guildhall that was being built on Market Square. He duly became a burgess and set up a successful trade in the town. From his base at number 24 Irongate, he designed all sorts of mechanical devices, including a sophisti-cated mechanical weather vane (perhaps built by the ironsmith Robert Bakewell) for his own house, and made numerous long-case clocks, instruments, watches, sundials and barometers, always 'beautifully made and closely fitted' and renowned for their accuracy, in some cases down to hundredths of a second. For the town he also rebuilt and improved the clock mechanism of All Saints in 1745.

It is even possible that he constructed a geared model of the Solar System (an 'orrery'), just like the one painted by Joseph Wright of Derby (see pages 38–9), and it has been conjectured that the kindly 'philosopher' depicted in Wright's painting might actually be Whitehurst. Wright painted Whitehurst's portrait, and Whitehurst certainly mingled with a large number of Enlightenment luminaries including the architect Joseph Pickford and the cartographer Peter Burdett. Through his association with the Birmingham-based Lunar Society, indeed, he got to know Benjamin Franklin, who stayed with Whitehurst twice in Derby. Also through that society Whitehurst became familiar with Josiah Wedgwood and indulged his interest in minerology by developing and perfecting minerals that Wedgwood could use in pottery glazes.

John Whitehurst of Derby was therefore a prominent Enlightenment figure. Such figures went on to have profound effects socially, intellectually, and technologically, which in turn fed in to Britain's early steps toward Industrial Revolution. Like many such figures, Whitehurst campaigned on issues such as the abolition of the slave trade. He was also an important figure in modern geological science, factory design, meteorology, and even domestic appliances. One such innovation was the perfection of what in effect was a hydraulic ram.

In later life, in the 1770s, Whitehurst took up several opportunities and lived in London, became a Fellow of the Royal Society, and studied the shape of the Earth by examining variations in gravity, a seemingly very modern activity. He died in 1788, without issue, but leaving behind an enormous scientific and intellectual legacy.

John Smith & Sons

Nicholas Smith, President, former Managing Director, Fourth Generation, and Archivist, John Smith & Sons

D ERBY has been the home of our family clock making business since 1856, and that of our fore-runners, the famous three generations of Whitehurst, also clockmakers, since 1735. Derby is a city which is famous for engineering in many forms. I was born into our family business in 1935, and I have climbed over 3,500 clock towers, including some with my father and some with my children. Our company uses various patented devices, usually dependent upon satellites, their synchronisation ensuring absolute accuracy.

In the early days, cuttings from newspapers, supplied by agencies, were used to find when a church or town hall was intending to install a clock. We have many books of these covering the late nineteenth century which show that a letter was sent

The University of Derby clock displayed proudly on the North Tower was designed to complement the structure's narrow width. It was installed in 2010 and cost £25,000.
SOURCE: NICHOLAS SMITH

5

and hopefully an order was subsequently received. Our fame gave us many orders during the busy late-Victorian and Edwardian periods. This included the clock in Trinity College, Cambridge (1910).

When I first joined the company in 1961, many of our products took too long to make and were expensive. No provision had been made for the retirement of employees or my extended family. We used the original old works which had wooden floors to protect the clocks' delicate teeth if somebody dropped a wheel. Despite, or perhaps because of, our traditional approach, we made many famous clocks throughout the world including: St Paul's Cathedral (1893); the highest altitude clock in the world at 12,000 feet in La Paz, Bolivia (1949); Salisbury Cathedral (1950s); Boeing's headquarters in Chicago (1990); and our largest mechanical clock of recent years in Ganzhou, China (2010). An excellent example of our work is that on the North Tower of the University of Derby, designed to suit the narrow width available.

There are fourth and fifth generation members of my family still actively involved as directors of the holding company, and my son, Professor Jonathan Smith, is also a director of the trading company. It is perhaps a healthy sign that both our very experienced chairman and managing director are non-family members. Our company is proud of our Derby heritage and its fame around the world. I do not think that there is a country in the world that does not have one of our clocks or features.

The original premises of John Smith & Sons, 27 Queen Street, photographed c.1952. The company has operated out of Derby since 1856.
SOURCE: NICHOLAS SMITH

Royal Crown Derby

Jacqueline Smith, Curator, Royal Crown Derby Museum

IT is my responsibility to look after the museum's collection of around 4,000 pieces of Derby porcelain dating from the 1750s up to the present day. The museum also holds an archive containing some very rare works on paper such as paintings, designs, and the company archives from 1877 onwards. Porcelain has been produced in Derby since about 1748. At this time porcelain was a new and luxurious material in this country and Derby was at the forefront of its manufacture and development.

William Duesbury built the reputation of the company by bringing it to the attention of London society. In 1770 he purchased the already established Chelsea factory and ran the two together until 1784 when he closed Chelsea and moved all production to Derby. The knowledge and talents of the two factories were combined, producing some of the finest gilders and enamellers in ceramic history. In 1774 Duesbury opened a showroom in Covent Garden which was visited by Queen Charlotte. This was a huge boost for the business because in the eighteenth century if royalty were buying something then the aristocracy wanted it too. In 1775 King George III honoured the factory by granting the Royal Warrant. The factory continued to gain the recogᵢnition of royalty and in 1890 Queen Victoria granted the use of 'Royal' in the title and the company became the 'Royal Crown Derby Porcelain Company'. In the twentieth century one of the company's most famous commissions was for the first‑class *à la carte* restaurant on the RMS *Titanic*.

Economically, Royal Crown Derby is important to the local community: it has been providing jobs for over 267 years and its

A Derby botanical plate featuring the Heber Percy pattern and a Mundi Rose, painted by celebrated artist William 'Quaker' Pegg, c.1815.

SOURCE: © ROYAL CROWN DERBY MUSEUM

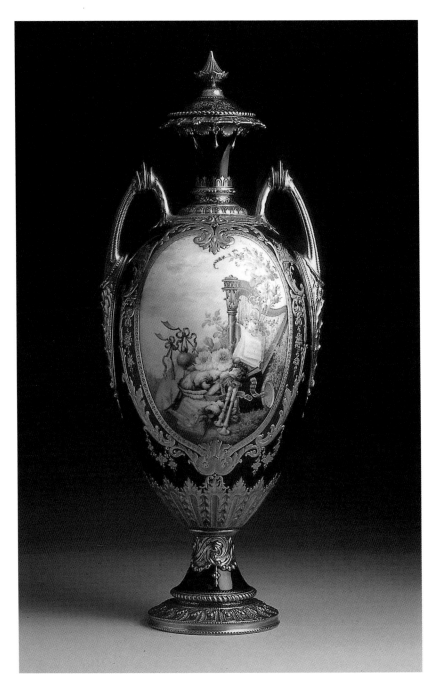

A vase designed and
painted by Desire
Leroy in 1899. It depicts
an array of musical
instruments covered with
various flowers.

products and heritage generate a sense of pride in the city. The company charts the
local history of manufacturing in Derby but it also plays a key role in the broader
context of ceramic history.

Derby Roundhouse

Maggie Tillson, Tourism Promotion Officer, Derby City Council

W HEN Derby Roundhouse underwent a huge redevelopment in 2009, we got excited at the prospect of doing tours to show off this magnificent place. The skills of tour guiding were soon picked up by the VisitDerby crew (Derby City Council's Tourism Team who are a very versatile bunch) and after planning the route and doing lots of research, off we went. Bookings soon flooded in, and over the years we have done tours for thousands of people from all over the world. The fact that Derby Roundhouse is the oldest remaining railway turning shed in the world is a huge asset for the city. We will never tire of seeing the look of wonder on visitors' faces when we enter the Roundhouse at the end of the tour. No words are needed as their jaws hit the floor looking up at the incredible beamed roof structure that once sheltered the likes of George Stephenson, father of the railways.

Early steam-driven railway locomotives did not have a reverse gear, and so roundhouses such as this in Derby, probably the first in the world, were constructed with turning circles to enable the engines to be rotated. This modern photograph shows the building in its role as part of Derby College.
SOURCE: © ALISON LOYDALL

Elements of the old and new architecture work together to create a unique aesthetic. The building is now Grade II listed.

SOURCE: © ALISON LOYDALL

7

It is great to see how the old and new architecture work in harmony at this site, now home to some lucky Derby College students. The mesmerising chameleon glass-fronted Matthew Kirtley building – named after one of the most important site superintendents in the 1840s – is a stark contrast to the red brick original, but one that reflects what we can construct nowadays. Visitors always marvel at its ever-changing colours during the tour, from the vivid orange outside, to the indoor purples and blues.

Although there are no locomotives left, there are many reminders of the site's heritage thanks to the clever and thoughtful design work of recent architects. Huge images of George Stephenson and Matthew Kirtley appear in the brand new college buildings which are named after these heroes of the railway industry. The huge glass walls in the carriage workshop, now the library, are adorned with the musical notes of the Railway Hornpipe to avoid the danger of walking into them nose first. The original rail tracks stay solid in the foundations and will remain a constant reminder of this site's amazing history. VisitDerby will certainly keep on showing visitors around this wonderful site which never fails to impress.

Railway Engineering at Derby

Alistair Hodge, local historian, lecturer, and publisher

W HEN the railways came to Derby it was big news: not just locally for the town (as it was then), but for the whole country. For Derby was one of the principal centres of the new railway network, a crucial hub of the then privately owned and operated Midland Railway, and a central part of the main east-coast line that was being built from London northward.

From the perspective of 2016, when Bombardier unveiled the rolling stock for the new London Crossrail scheme that it would be constructing at its famous old Litchurch Lane works in Derby, it is difficult to conceive of what a big story the coming of the railways really was for the town. Not only did railways provide an efficient, fast new mode of transport for the people and industries of the town, but they opened up new broad horizons. For the first time people could travel far

The Running Shed at the Derby Locomotive Works, c.1903. This was one of three sheds used for locomotive maintenance and storage.

SOURCE: SCIENCE & SOCIETY PICTURE LIBRARY © PAST PIX

and wide at reasonable cost and with relative ease, while all sorts of commodities, manufactured goods, and produce could be transported hither and thither to an extent that would have been inconceivable to earlier generations. Culturally, too, it was a step-change, as newspapers, magazines and books, many of them from London, could now be distributed quickly and efficiently. W. H. Smith was quick to realise the potential, and quickly negotiated a contract to open bookstalls on railway platforms (by 1870 there were over 500 across the country).

In Derby the effect of the railways was more profound than almost anywhere. The town's central location and distance from London made it a logical place to establish an engineering base. A whole new regional industry was born, in locomotive and carriage design, manufacturing, and repair. Already the town had several important and well-regarded iron foundries that could produce castings of various sorts, so there were plenty of skilled and experienced metalworkers able to turn their hands to building and repairing the large numbers of locomotives and carriages needed for the quickly expanding rail network.

At various times the works in Derby produced a full range of rolling stock. Locomotives had been built in the town from the 1840s, with James Eastwood & Sons employing several hundred people and exporting engines to France, Russia, the USA and Australia. The first locomotives to be built in-house by the Midland

Constructing a carriage roof on the floor of Derby Carriage & Wagon Works, November 1922. Take a closer look at this image, including the complex carpentry joints on the sides of the carriage, and the hand tools lying about, and one quickly realises that carriage manufacturing required significant wood- as well as metal-working skills until well into the twentieth century.

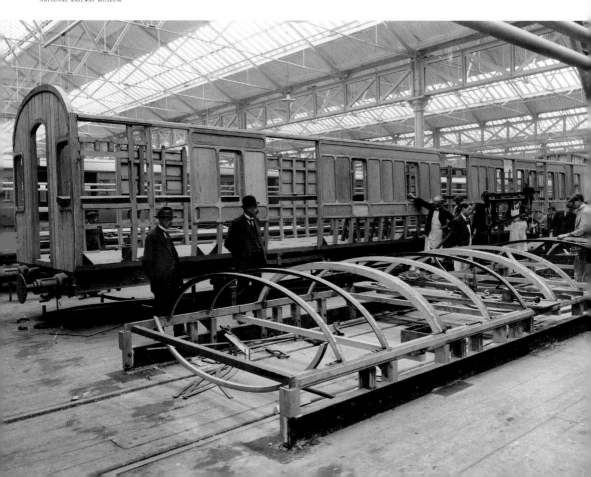

The upholstery trimming shop at the London, Midland & Scottish Railways Carriage & Wagon Works, Derby, 12 June 1936. In this one room alone around 45 men (and no women) are at work. At centre right we see the supervisor, with bowler hat, watch chain, suit, and hands behind his back, with the nearby workers, in flat caps, watching his progress along the lines of benches as he checks their work. A fascinating snapshot of social history.

SOURCE: SCIENCE & SOCIETY PICTURE LIBRARY ©
NATIONAL RAILWAY MUSEUM

were produced in 1851, under the able direction of Matthew Kirtley. Kirtley was a remarkable railway pioneer. He was present at the opening of the Stockton–Darlington, and of the Liverpool to Manchester Railway in 1830, and went on to become chief designer at the 'Loco' works in Derby for almost thirty years.

A new Carriage and Wagon Works was opened in 1876, and Derby's capacity for the production of carriages and wagons grew enormously. At its peak, the works could produce 350 carriages and up to 10,000 wagons a year. Eventually thousands of skilled workers — not just iron founders and metal workers, but carpenters, upholsterers, and draughtsmen in the Locomotive Drawing Office nearby — would find well-paid employment in a range of facilities near the main lines, behind the station itself, on Cotton Lane, and on Litchurch Lane, producing rolling stock for use on British, Imperial, and overseas railways around the globe.

For decades the Derby railway works was a hugely important employer in the town. During the Second World War they contributed to the war effort by making wings for Hurricane fighter planes and light tanks, while foundries elsewhere in the town made armaments of various sorts. Following the war came nationalisation and the works operated, for 20 years, as British Rail Engineering Limited.

Locomotives being assembled in Derby works' erecting shop, 23 July 1910. Derby works produced its first new locomotive in 1851 and production expanded rapidly. By the 1900s the works was producing carriages and wagons, as well as locomotives. It covered 80 acres and employed over 4,000 people.

The Litchurch Works is all that remains of this extensive network of engineering works, albeit still a hugely important one for the regional economy, with a large skilled workforce currently producing rolling stock for London and elsewhere, and the works under the ownership of Bombardier Transportation. This Canadian company, whose transportation headquarters moved in 2001 to Berlin so that they could tap more easily into Europe, the world's most important market for railway rolling stock, took over the Derby works in the same year.

In the early days of rail, locomotives and carriages were quite distinct entities, but now the Derby works specialises in the manufacture of self-powered diesel or electric 'multiple units'. These are built to order for clients overseas and particularly in London, for the Underground, Metronet, Crossrail and other rail initiatives. Bombardier is investing in driverless technologies, too, a far cry from the very first locomotives and rolling stock that were designed by Matthew Kirtley 150 years ago.

Despite all the changes, rail engineering remains one of Derby's oldest and most distinctive economic success stories.

Rolls-Royce

Amy Drew, Assistant Editor, The Derby Yearbook

ROLLS-ROYCE have been making an impact on Derby since 1908 when Charles Rolls and Henry Royce opened their custom-built factory on Nightingale Road. The factory initially built the Silver Ghost, called the 'greatest car in the world' by *Autocar* magazine. The success of this car made Rolls-Royce famous around the world and helped put Derby on the map as a centre for engineering excellence. The Rolls-Royce name is most famous for manufacturing luxury cars and jet engines, but they also build engines for submarines. The submarine arm of the business is based in Derby and their engines power the Royal Navy's fleet of nuclear powered submarines, including the new Astute class vessels.

During the First World War, Rolls-Royce built aircraft engines for the newly established Royal Air Force. Henry Royce designed and produced his first aero engine, the Eagle, which was built in Derby and powered the Vickers Vimy bombers

Rolls-Royce Silver Ghost, 1909. This is one of the earliest Silver Ghost motor cars to have been made. Built in 1909, with chassis number 1119, it was used continuously until 1929 by the Marquis of Cholmondeley. This type of Silver Ghost was in production until 1925. It is fitted with a Hooper landaulet body, which is supported on a stiff chassis frame of channel-section steel girders. The six-cylinder 40/50 hp water-cooled engine has a cylinder capacity of 7.428 litres. The car could run at a speed of 34 mph at 1,000 rpm in top gear.

SOURCE: SCIENCE & SOCIETY PICTURE LIBRARY © SCIENCE MUSEUM

during the war. This was also the engine that in June 1919 powered the modified
Vimy on the first successful transatlantic flight. During the Second World War,
Derby was the main hub for the manufacture of Rolls-Royce Merlin engines that
would famously power the Spitfire, Hurricane, Lancaster bomber, Mosquito, and
Mustang aircraft. Over 30,000 Merlin engines were built in Derby, the highest
number of any of the British factories supplying the engine. The Merlin is possibly
the only engine that has become a household name in the United Kingdom, which
is testament to its significance in the war effort.

Today Rolls-Royce is one of the world's largest manufacturers of engines for civil,
corporate, and defence aircraft. Derby's Sinfin plant, that replaced the Nightingale
Road factory, employs around 14,000 people and makes a huge economic impact
on the city. It is Rolls-Royce's largest UK site where they design, assemble, and test
Trent jet engines; Trent XWB engines are one of the most efficient large aircraft
engines on the market and are used on all Airbus A350 XWB aircraft. Derby also
designs and produces the Trent 1000 engines that are used to power around half of
Boeing's fleet of 787 Dreamliners. Next time that you are aboard an aeroplane, it is
possible that its engine was built just down the road, in Derby.

Rolls-Royce Merlin engine. The engine was a vital component of the planes, such as the Spitfire, Hurricane and Mosquito, used during the Second World War.

Rolls-Royce Conway jet engine. Rolls-Royce began developing the world's first turbofan engine in the 1940s. Despite insolvency in 1971 because of difficulties with the innovative RB211 turbofan design, the company thrives to this day.

Joseph Wright of Derby

Lucy Bamford, Senior Curator of Art, Derby Museums and Art Gallery

I WAS INTRODUCED to the work of Joseph Wright as a child during visits to the Museum and Art Gallery with my family. I have loved Wright's paintings and drawings ever since, and so looking after the collection of his work at Derby Museums feels like a dream. I was awed then and I continue to be inspired by the fact that Wright was from Derby. That he made some of his most visionary and unforgettable paintings here makes their meaning even more powerful for me. My job involves caring for and preserving this amazing collection for future generations, and I see one of my most important roles as that of a Joseph Wright ambassador, sharing my passion for the artist's work and supporting others (especially Derbeians) in discovering its wonders and significance for themselves.

Joseph Wright was born on 3 September 1734 at the family home on Irongate in Derby. At the age of 17, he left Derby for London to train under Thomas Hudson, one of the most celebrated portrait painters of the mid-eighteenth century. When he returned to his home town in 1758, Wright quickly earned himself a strong local following with his honest, yet sensitive,

A Philosopher Giving that Lecture on the Orrery, in which a Lamp is put in the Place of the Sun, by Joseph Wright, oil on canvas, exhibited 1766. This is perhaps Wright's most famous work, perfectly encapsulating the Enlightenment.

Fire in Rome, by Joseph
Wright, pen with bistre
wash on toned paper,
1774.
SOURCE: © 2017 DERBY
MUSEUMS TRUST

portraits. Portraiture continued to provide him with an income throughout his forty-year career, but Wright had ambitions beyond its narrow confines.

From around 1754, he started to explore painting groups of people gathered around an activity who were lit by a candle or lamp. The result was a series of eye-catching scenes — rich in the colours and contrast of deep shadow and bright light — that shot Wright to fame. *A Philosopher giving that Lecture on the Orrery, in which a Lamp is put in the Place of the Sun* (c.1766), was one of these paintings. It is easy to see why Wright has since come to be known as a 'painter of light'. Some view the painting as an icon of Wright's times and his association with key members of the intellectual movement known as the Enlightenment. *The Orrery* is an undisputed masterpiece of British art and the jewel in Derby Museums' collection.

Wright's interests, like those of the artists, poets, industrialists, philosophers, and scientists with whom he socialised, were wide-ranging. His art followed suit to include subjects from both historical and modern literature, current events, and landscape painting, not to mention portraiture. When other artists were specialising

in one aspect of painting, Wright was exploring all that the world and its ideas had to offer his creative drive. While many artists chose to live and work in London, then the centre of the art world, Wright remained in Derby, save for a few brief trips to Liverpool, Italy, Bath, and the Lake District. It is for this reason that he came to be known in his own lifetime as 'Wright of Derby', a nickname that has stuck to this day.

Joseph Wright Study Room

Matt Edwards, Curator of Visual Art and the Joseph Wright
Study Centre, Derby Museums and Art Gallery

I BEGAN WORKING at Derby Museums in 1999 after studying fine art at the University of Derby. It was shortly after that I also began working as a conservation bookbinder originally employed to care for the collections in local studies libraries throughout Derbyshire. I continued to work in a variety of roles at the museum and it was therefore a privilege to assume the post of Curator of Visual Art and the Joseph Wright Study Centre in 2014. The study room opened that year and is a place where visitors can access the Joseph Wright archive which includes over 300 drawings and sketches, more than 50 engravings, letters, and a large library of art and local history books. The drawings and prints are stored in specially designed drawers allowing many to be viewed during any visit.

In the collection you can discover Joseph Wright's earliest known drawings — from when he was about 16 years old. In the artist's early studies of costume, the soft tones of silk, satin, and lacework are suggested using only delicate black and white chalks on blue paper. These works form a portfolio used by the artist when commissioned to paint his fine portraits. Many of the drawings are from Wright's journey through France and Italy on what was termed 'The Grand Tour'. It was during this trip that Wright sketched the classical art, people, and places he encountered on his travels. He returned to England in 1775 with a passion for landscape painting and the later studies reflect his love of Derbyshire, particularly Dovedale, which was already a tourist destination in the eighteenth century and attracted artists and writers.

A rare collection of original letters reveal how the artist thoroughly researched his subjects. In many cases such information was not readily available in the eighteenth century. To his friend, the poet William Hayley, concerning his painting *The Widow of an Indian Chief Watching the Arms of her Deceased Husband* (1783–84) he wrote: 'The scenery, the Habiliments of War are finished in the Indian picture but

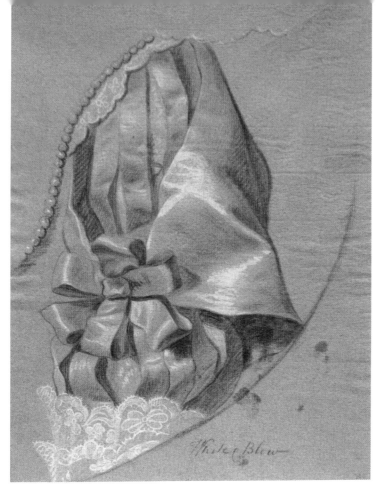

Study of a Woman's Arm in a Van Dyck Dress with Pearl Embroidered Neckline, c.1755–57. This early piece by Wright explores the soft tones of silk, satin and lacework, and was created using black and white chalk on blue paper.

Dovedale, watercolour, c.1780–85. When Wright returned from 'The Grand Tour' in 1775 he had developed a passion for landscape painting. His later works often depicted the idyllic Derbyshire countryside.

the figure for want of knowing the Dress of the Mourner is only an outline. I wrote to you about it, but I suppose it escaped your notice. If you can give me any hints I shall be obliged to you.' These works were previously held in stores to be viewed only by appointment. In taking a new open access approach with the Study Room we allow all our visitors a broader view of the life and work of Joseph Wright and eighteenth-century Derby during what is termed the Age of Enlightenment.

Derby Silk Mill

Jordan Reynolds, Assistant Editor, The Derby Yearbook

T OWERING ABOVE the river Derwent, the Silk Mill stands on the site of Britain's first factory. This mill was built for the Lombe brothers between 1717 and 1721 to house machines that twisted (or 'threw') silk into thread.

The idea of textile mills in northern Britain is now so familiar to us – of cotton mills in Derbyshire and Lancashire, woollen mills in Yorkshire, and hosiery mills in Nottinghamshire – that it is difficult to appreciate the remarkable novelty and importance of Lombes' achievement and the extent of their contribution to Britain's industrial development in the eighteenth century.

Silk, then as now, was a luxury product that commanded a high price, and the technology for its economical production was a closely guarded secret. By the late sixteenth century, by far the most advanced silk-throwing machinery and technology were to be found in northern Italy.

Enter John Lombe, an enterprising young man from a textile family. We do not know exactly when and why he decided upon his hazardous journey to Piedmont, but he may well have been aware of the enterprising and ultimately unsuccessful Cotchett's silk mill project on the river Derwent in Derby that had

Print of the Silk Mill by J. Nixon, 1774. Built between 1718 and 1722 when John and Thomas Lombe introduced Italian technology. The main silk mill that contained the twelve rotating silk-throwing drums came to be known as the 'Italian works'.

The Silk Mill as it looks in 2017, in the process of becoming the Museum of Making – a project due to be completed by 2020. Most of the fabric of the building post-dates the huge fire a century ago, but the historical significance of the building remains huge.

SOURCE: © ALISON LOYDALL

been built in 1704. In cloak-and-dagger circumstances John spent many months working and observing the Italian silk-making machinery, reputedly making secret sketches from memory and drawing them up later. However it transpired, we know that a year later he and some workers he persuaded to join him from Italy had returned to Derby, leased the water rights to the Derwent from the good burgesses of the town, and set about constructing the world-famous Derby Silk Mill right next to Cotchett's mill on a small island in the river.

Hardly surprisingly the Italians were livid. A reward was offered for the capture of Lombe, and later the king of Piedmont Sardinia banned the export of raw silk to try to force Lombe out of business. It was one of the most infamous early examples of industrial espionage, an outrageous theft of technological know-how

Portrait of Jedediah Strutt (1726–96) by Joseph Wright of Derby. Strutt was the inventor of the 'Derby rib' framework knitting machine, which could produce ribbed stockings that were better fitting. He also partnered Richard Awkwright at Cromford, opened a silk mill of his own in Derby, and, most importantly, was the founder of the cotton spinning mills at Belper and Milford.

that was made all the more outrageous by the fact that Lombe went on to secure a 14-year patent for the 'invention' that he was now passing off as his own in England. He even secured £14,000 compensation from Parliament when the patent expired.

Relief sculpture of John Lombe on Exeter Bridge, Derby.

SOURCE: © CARNEGIE

John Lombe did not live long to enjoy his notoriety or his success. By 1722, just months after the mill opened, he was dead. One legend goes that when the king of Piedmont Sardinia heard of the Lombe brothers' success, he sent a female assassin to kill John in retribution for his copying of the machine design.

Why was this mill so revolutionary? Only in part because it transformed the manufacture of silk thread of high quality and low cost. The real significance of the Derby Silk Mill is that it has a strong case to be Britain's first true factory, a prototype for the dozens and then hundreds of similar textile mills that would be built across Britain and the world in later decades.

For this mill was the first true industrial enterprise in which large numbers of people worked at set times of the day tending and minding machinery (in this case at least 12 large, drum-shaped silk-throwing machines and many winding machines on the floors above) that were all turned by a single power source, in this case a massive waterwheel that was driven by the waters of the fast-moving Derwent.

Despite the Italian embargo of silk supplies, Thomas Lombe took over the running of the mill following John's death, and it appears to have been a great commercial success, with Thomas reputedly being worth £120,000 when he died, a truly enormous sum at the time.

After the death of William Lombe in 1739, the mill was sold by his widow. From there the mill was passed from businessman to businessman, each using the premises for the manufacture of silk. In 1908, the connection to the silk trade was severed when F.W. Hampshire & Company, the chemists, decided to use the site to produce cough medicines. This peace was short lived. On 5 December 1910, a fire broke out in the early hours of the morning in the adjacent property which quickly spread and engulfed the Silk Mill. The east side of the mill collapsed into the Derwent and the interior was completely destroyed, despite the best efforts of the fire department. The effects of this fire can still be seen today. It was not until 29 November 1974 that the building was adapted into the museum that now stands as a monument to Derby's rich industrial heritage.

All that survives of the original early eighteenth-century building are some massive stone foundation arches.

Joseph Pickford

Jordan Reynolds, Assistant Editor, The Derby Yearbook

NAMED after its architect, Joseph Pickford, there is an elegant Georgian town house that nestles comfortably among the old buildings and cobbled streets of Friar Gate. Built in 1770, Pickford's House is a splendid example of the divide between master and servant from the eighteenth century until the twentieth. This house is now an important museum in the city.

Joseph Pickford was a highly talented architect, generally reckoned to be one of the best provincial architects of the Georgian era. He was born in Warwickshire in 1734, but moved to London following his father's death. Pickford gained a highly practical education and training first as a stonemason with his uncle, and worked with him in the capital for about a decade. He then went on to study and train in architecture. In 1760, Pickford moved to Derby where he became the agent of architect David Hiorne. He was married to Mary Wilkins and designed the house, now known as Pickford's House Museum, as his family home.

Pickford's House is far from his only architectural masterpiece in Derby and the region. Perhaps most importantly, tucked behind a red-brick wall on King Street is the magnificent, recently restored St Helen's House. This building, whose original façade is intact, is the finest Palladian town house in the region, and one of the best in the country. Built in 1776–77 as a home for entertaining large numbers of guests for local alderman John Gisborne, it was later occupied by William Strutt, son of Jedediah. The house, appropriately enough, was adorned with several paintings by Joseph Wright, while some of the finest craftsmen in the country were employed to build fireplaces, a superb wrought-iron stair-rail, and other embellishments such as fine plasterwork. For a hundred years until the 1960s St Helen's House was home to Derby School, and it has now been converted to offices.

In the eighteenth century Derby was known as a fine Georgian town, and Pickford's building was responsible in no small measure for this reputation. He designed the Assembly Rooms and a house on Cornmarket for Hugh Bateman, as well as new almshouses on Full Street. Shortly before his death in 1782, Pickford completed the enlargement of Darley Hall. Pickford worked across the Midlands designing a variety of buildings. Pickford had a number of friends from the

Lunar Society, including painter Joseph Wright, and the inventor John Whitehurst. Pickford is thought to have designed Whitehurst's home in Queen Street, Derby. His connections to regional Enlightenment figures included Josiah Wedgwood, and it was therefore no surprise that he was also asked to design the red-brick Etruria Hall for Wedgwood.

Pickford's House is one of the architect's designs that can be visited readily today. Now a Grade I listed building owned by Derby City Council, it has been converted into a museum so that members of the public can enjoy an educational insight into the Georgian era. Without asking for permission the council had the chimney replaced, along with some of the floors and walls. However, the house still offers a genuine journey into the depths of life in a Georgian townhouse. From the luxurious dining room, filled with paintings and decorated with fine woodwork; to the plain scullery at the rear of the building; to the bucolic garden at the rear of the house, still bustling with era appropriate flora, Pickford's House is truly remarkable.

Pickford's House Museum of Georgian Life and Costume, 41 Friar Gate. The museum was established in 1988 and shows the accommodation of a late Georgian professional.
SOURCE: © ALISON LOYDALL

The Cathedral of All Saints

Alex Rock, Development Officer, Derby Cathedral

G RADE I LISTED Derby Cathedral is an icon of the city. Churches on this site have given the people of Derby a place to gather, debate, and develop for over a thousand years. The building houses key aspects of the heritage of the city, county, and diocese; its collection tells the hidden stories of Derby's innovators. A major church was founded on the site of the Cathedral in AD 943; nothing of this

A view up Irongate to what is often regarded as the finest church tower in Derbyshire, the early sixteenth-century tower of All Saints, Derby, designed in Perpendicular Gothic style.

SOURCE: © ALISON LOYDALL

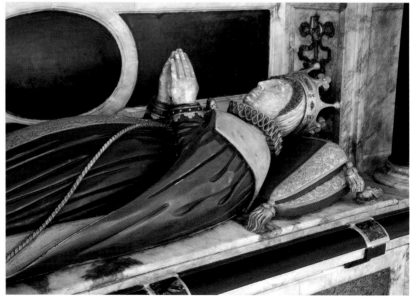

The mayor's pew is fronted by decorated ironwork that incorporates a painting of the city badge, a stag enclosed by park palings. The ironwork is by the renowned Derby ironsmith Robert Bakewell.

SOURCE © CARNEGIE

Effigy of Bess of Hardwick. John Smythson designed this alabaster figure for Bess six years before her death in 1607. She is interred in the vault below the former Cavendish chapel.

SOURCE © CARNEGIE

earlier building is thought to remain. All Saints (or 'All Hallows', as it was known) was one of three pre-Conquest churches of Derby. Of these, Derby Cathedral is the last working place of worship. Its Tudor tower, erected between 1510 and 1530, is the second-tallest bell tower in England, housing the world's oldest working ring of ten bells. It was thought that, aside from foundation stones still visible on the south side of the Cathedral exterior, nothing of the fourteenth-century church remained. However, during recent works, a sizeable portion of medieval stonework was found within the walls.

Some of the Cathedral's monuments date from this era, including the alabaster memorial slab to Sub-Dean Lawe from the mid-1400s, and the 1530s wooden effigy of Sub-Dean Johnson. Older still is the fourteenth-century grave slab that was reused for the Enlightenment painter Joseph Wright of Derby. In 1600, a grand monument to Bess of Hardwick was built in the nave. This strengthened an on-going relationship with the Cavendish family. Many were buried here, including Georgiana, Duchess of Devonshire, and Henry Cavendish, responsible for the discovery of hydrogen.

By the early 1700s, the majority of the church was demolished, with only the Tudor tower left. With the congregation forced into funding a rebuilt Church, James Gibbs was chosen as the architect. Gibbs is also responsible for St Martin-in-the-Fields in London, Cambridge's Senate House, and the Radcliffe Camera at Oxford University. A local blacksmith, Robert Bakewell, was commissioned in 1730 to make the wrought-iron screen. The architecture of the interior has remained

Wooden effigy of Sub-Dean Johnson, dating from the 1530s. In Derbyshire there is a large number of fine alabaster tomb effigies, but inevitably wooden ones have lasted less well, and this is a rare survivor of the type.
SOURCE © CARNEGIE

largely unaltered, with only the furnishings and floor out-of-keeping with the Enlightenment Church.

Innovators of the twentieth century associated with the Cathedral include the surrealist Ceri Richards, responsible for the two abstract stained glass east windows. The work of the acclaimed Sir Ninian Comper can be seen in the Cathedral's extension. The Cathedral is home to the largest collection of church textiles produced by Leonard Childs, the celebrated Modernist textiles designer who ran Derby Cathedral's Embroidery Workshop from 1955 until his death in 2003. The Cathedral is an important icon in the city and is open to all as a place of quiet and reflection in a busy world.

The tower of the church of All Saints was preserved when the nave of the church (seen here) was designed and rebuilt in the 1720s and 1730s. Gibbs was a famous architect of the age and created a wonderfully light interior, with Tuscan columns. Gibbs also designed the wrought-iron screen, which was built by Robert Bakewell (though only the central parts are original).

Derby's Peregrine Falcons

Nick Brown, Derby Cathedral Peregrine Project, Derbyshire Wildlife Trust

PEREGRINE FALCONS are normally birds of mountains, moors, and coasts that nest on remote cliffs. Following a dip in population size in the 1950s there was an increase in the United Kingdom's peregrine population, and young birds began to look inland for cliffs on which to nest. To a peregrine, Derby Cathedral's wonderful 212 foot tower is essentially a cliff, and a pair of wild peregrines discovered it in 2004–05. However, there were no flat ledges on which they could lay eggs, so in the spring of 2006, a wooden nesting platform was set up on the east side of the tower to accommodate them. The birds immediately adopted it and raised young that year, and in every subsequent year, to much media acclaim. Derbyshire Wildlife Trust, which now manages the project with the active support of the Cathedral, runs a series of 'Watch Points' on Cathedral Green in May and June so that anyone can see the birds up close through telescopes.

In 2007, web cameras were fixed to the nest so that the intimate details of the peregrines' breeding cycle could be seen worldwide. The cameras and accompanying blog have now been viewed over four million times and from over 70 countries, really putting Derby on the map. The peregrines lay their eggs at the end of March or early April. They hatch in early May and the chicks fledge mid-June. The parent birds stay around all year and can often be seen sitting on the lettering on the tall Jurys Inn building

Peregrine falcon in front of the tower in which it nests.

SOURCE: NICK BROWN ©
STUART WHITEHEAD

nearby. Peregrines feed exclusively on other birds which they catch in flight and analysis of their prey shows that they feed on a wide variety of birds, even capturing some at night using the floodlighting. The young leave Derby in late summer and so far 37 have fledged. Most have been colour ringed so that we can keep track of them. One of our females is nesting on a cliff in Yorkshire and another has spent the last two winters at Rutland Water.

Hindu Temple Geeta Bhawan

Soshain Bali, Trustee, Multi-Faith Centre

I N THE 1960s a number of Hindu families met at one another's houses for community gatherings. As the community grew, meetings were held to fundraise enough money for the purchase of a terraced house on Normanton Road in the 1970s.

With growing community requirements, a purpose built modern building over two floors with a car park was established on Pear Tree Road in 2008. The Hindu Temple reflects the traditional family ethos to provide a plethora of community functions including: religious and cultural welfare, education, charity, health and safety, festivities, dance, and yoga exercises. On the ground floor a spacious hall with catering facilities is used for community festivals such as Diwali and wedding functions. The Mandir is on the first floor; Hindu deities enshrine the beautifully decorated and hand carved inner sanctum of the Mandir to offer their blessings in serene surroundings.

The Mandir Aarti and Puja are performed twice a day by the priest, yoga classes are held three times a week, there is a senior citizen luncheon club on a Tuesday, and modern and traditional dance classes are also taught. An educational block provides space for Hindi classes and there is an additional small function room with a kitchen.

The inner temple of the Geeta Bhawan on Pear Tree Road.
SOURCE: © SOSHAIN BALI

Sikh Gurdwara

Dr Hardial Singh Dhillon, Sikh Advisor to the University of Derby

16

G URU ARJAN DEV GURDWARA came into existence in the 1960s when a few committed Sikhs bought two adjoining houses on Malcolm Street and turned them into a place of worship. Nowadays, the Gurdwara stands tall on Stanhope Street with a building constructed by the help of donations from the Sikh congregation. The present Sikh population in Derby is around 20,000.

The Sikh religion focuses on the eternal, formless Lord and the spiritual goodness in people; Oneness of Lord and oneness of humanity are the basic principles of Sikhi. A Sikh means 'a learner' and therefore Sikhs remain open to broadening their horizons and accepting all as children of the same God, regardless of the differences that may exist among people of different religions.

Every day, the Guru Granth Sahib (the Sikh Scripture) is brought from its private room and opened randomly on a page where a quote of the day is taken and projected on the screen in front of the main hall. It is taken to mean as a divine commandment for everybody to read and act upon. On special occasions, there is a continuous reading (known as 'an Akhand Paath') of the Guru Granth Sahib (the Sikh Holy Scripture), starting on Friday and ending on Sunday morning by anyone who is an amritdhari (an initiated) Sikh; this is done for the benefit of

View from inside the Sikh Temple on Stanhope Street.
SOURCE: © ALISON LOYDALL

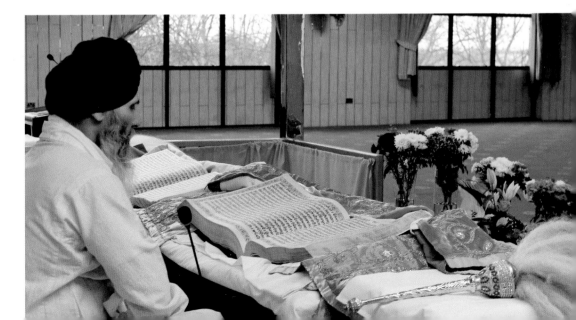

The Sikh Temple, which was constructed with the help of donations from the congregation.

SOURCE: © ALISON LOYDALL

all, whosoever wishes to listen; a reader is changed after every two hours regularly over those 48 hours.

Apart from traditional worship, there are several activities offered at the Gurdwara such as Gurmat classes to help the younger generation learn about the Guru's teachings. Other activities include kirtan (music) and gatka (martial arts) classes. The outreach food distribution is a daily happening, wherein volunteers prepare food in the kitchen at the Gurdwara and distribute it to the needy. The slogan for that being 'with langar, no hunger'. Halls may also be used for events such as weddings. No matter what the occasion may be, Guru Arjan Dev Gurdwara is a warm and welcoming place infused with compassion and serenity.

St Mary's Catholic Church

Fran Wickes, Parish Catechetical Coordinator, St Mary's Church

S T MARY'S Catholic Church is a building of national and international architectural renown. It was the first important parish church designed by the
pioneering exponent of the neo-Gothic revival, Augustus Pugin. Opening
in October 1839, it is associated with a long line of other eminent designers,
builders, and architects. George Myers, the celebrated master craftsman, was
responsible for building St Mary's. John Hardman, the ecclesiastical metalwork
and stained glass designer, furnished the church. Herbert Minton created
the original tiles. The only significant alterations to the building have
been the addition of the Lady Chapel, Pieta Chapel and vestries in 1855
by Pugin's son, Edward.

Throughout its history St Mary's has undergone extensive restoration work
to preserve it for future generations, the most significant being between 1927 and
1931 when the parish priest, Mons Charles Payne, led a heroic effort to prevent

St Mary's Church.
According to Dr
Wiseman at the church's
opening in 1838, 'without
exception the most
magnificent thing that
Catholics have done in
modern times in this
country'.
SOURCE: © ALISON LOYDALL

Stained glass window in
St Mary's church.

The nave of St Mary's
Church: the first
important parish church
designed by Augustus
Pugin, who is perhaps
best known for designing
the interior of the Palace
of Westminster.

St Mary's Church:
carving of the death of
Christ.

the collapse of the church due to defective stonework. In 2016 the Lady Chapel underwent a £250,000 programme of works to restore much of its original beauty that had been lost to the painter's brush in the 1970s. Many Catholic families are proud to have held all their baptisms, marriages, and funerals within the walls of St Mary's for generations. Derby now has a full complement of Catholic parish churches, but the older members of these congregations still remember a time when St Mary's was the 'Mother Church.' Each Sunday they clubbed together to pay for a taxi to bring a St Mary's priest to a hall or room they had rented for Mass to be said. The affection for St Mary's runs deep and she continues to be a vibrant parish church and a beacon for the faith and prayer life of the people of Derby.

St Mary's Church:
Crucifixion triptych.
SOURCE: © JENNY WELCH

Islam in Derby

Idris Sadat, Islamic Scholar, Minister of Religion

I AM a local Islamic Scholar who has studied and obtained a degree in Islamic Theology. I have by the grace of Allah been blessed to teach multiple divine Islamic sciences and doctrines such as commentary of the Quran, Hadith, and Jurisprudence. I hold a revered, esteemed, and influential role as a local scholar in Derby. My job is to pass verdicts (Islamic rulings), teach the youngsters in the community, and conduct speeches, and so on. Any issues that arise in the community are presented before me. Holding such a role necessitates strong influence.

There are many mosques within the vicinity of Derby. However, only two are purpose built. One is located near the city centre while the other is situated in Normanton. Other than prayer, there are many services provided at these mosques such as nurseries, private schools, supplementary schools, school visits, community visits, and other activities.

The holy month of Ramadan is sentimental and divine to Muslims. It holds great significance in Islam since it is when the Holy Quran was revealed. Understandably, the Muslims in Derby passionately prepare for this blessed month. Public gatherings are held in order to prepare the general mass for the inauguration of Ramadan and during which, one can sense a feeling of unity, mutual love, and peace. The number of worshippers in the mosques dramatically increases during this period and people also congregate to partake in opening their fasts and the nocturnal prayer.

I would like the non-Muslims of not just Derby, but the whole world, to know that Islam is a religion that strongly advocates peace, good character, morals, and ethics, simultaneously condemning violence, terror, extremism, and hatred. I would also recommend that people read the life of our Noble Apostle Muhammad, peace be upon him, since his life serves as a perfect example and sets precedent in all the aforementioned traits. There is an alarming need for constructive education rather than mere consuming of the media.

The Multi-Faith Centre

Emeritus Professor Jonathan Powers, Former Honorary Vice-President,
Project Champion, and Acting Chairman, Multi-Faith Centre

T HIS is the first religious building initiated by members of seven major religions. Though 'secular', the university owes its origins in 1851 to Bishop Lonsdale of Lichfield, and in 1990 a representative committee was set up to guide policy on religious observance. With Paul Weller (later Professor of Inter-Religious Relations), I was keen that any religious facilities should serve the educational purpose of promoting mutual understanding through dialogue. Paul was overseeing a ground-breaking project of dialogical scholarship – a directory of all the major religious groups in the United Kingdom, with negotiated accounts of their history, doctrine, and organisation. Thanks to Michael Hall (later Deputy Vice-Chancellor) in 1993, *Religions in the UK* sealed our reputation for inter-religious dialogue.

The committee (chaired by Dr Hardial Singh Dhillon) embraced the concept of a shared facility. We spent three years hammering out the design brief and rules for use: this was the start of real dialogue. It must suggest 'depth' and 'transcendence' yet not be like any known religious building. We needed time-shared spaces to promote understanding and mutual respect, where people of all faiths, and those without, were welcome. We held an architectural competition on 24 October 1996.

The clear winner was Mark Swindells, a young architect who entered 'just for the experience'. The depth of analysis shown in his imaginative 'Village of Spaces' was acclaimed unanimously. Having agreed to provide the prime site, the University Council challenged us to raise the money from the faith communities themselves. Leading figures from nine world faith traditions gave support and we engaged Compton International to work with us.

Robert Astick managed the campaign, which was chaired by Sir Harold Haywood (former Director of the Prince's Trust). The Mayor launched the campaign on 24 November 1999, with a target of £2.5 million. I became 'frontman' and project champion. Despite years of obtaining millions from funding bodies, I had never done fundraising face-to-face. Under Robert's guidance I learned how it could be a really positive force for the sharing of commitment and enthusiasm. The Millennium Commission invited us to bid for matched funding. The first chairman of the trust was the Rt Revd Jonathan Bailey (Lord Bishop of

Derby). I worked as his executive vice-chairman until he retired. We were rocked by the closure of Religious Studies at the university due to financial pressures, but the project had the strong support of the Vice-Chancellor. I acquired the directory project, its resources, and its manager, Eileen Fry. In 2001 we published the third edition, and Eileen became our first director.

Fundraising involved a lot of footwork, but all communities contributed. Having selected Bluestone as our contractor, we were given 6 October 2003 as the deadline to start. But as costs rose, the money we were raising fell back. In 'value engineering exercises', Mark Swindells completely redesigned the building twice. The walls of his final single storey building echo the Ring of Brodgar sheltering a roof garden. On the deadline Eileen dug symbolically into the turf, and on 22 December 2003, primary school children from our seven major faith traditions laid the foundation stone. With a host of awards, the building was officially opened by the Duke of Gloucester on 19 October 2005. Representatives of twenty different religious (and non-religious) traditions attended. Under successive directors (Eileen Fry, Carrie Edwards, and Dr Phil Henry) the Centre has been at the forefront of promoting religious dialogue. There is no longer any equivocation about the importance of such work. Our golden rule is to listen to others as you wish them to listen to you. The journey itself is the goal.

The University of Derby

Emeritus Professor Jonathan Powers DL Hon DUniv

T HE YEAR 2017 marks the 25th anniversary of Derbyshire College of Higher
Education becoming a university – the only college alongside the former
polytechnics.

It was an extraordinary collective achievement. We had been hit by two disasters
in 1991. In January, we suffered Derby's biggest fire since World War II. Then, in
December, Kenneth Clarke declared there would be no more polytechnics. Aspiring
colleges would need powers for research degrees, which few polytechnics ever
obtained from the Council for National Academic Awards (CNAA).

The Kirtley Building at
Kedleston Road on fire, 7
January 1991.

BISHOP LONSDALE'S
BIBLE

OWL OF ATHENA
ABOUT TO FLY

TUDOR ROSE OF
DERBYSHIRE

STAG
GORGED WITH PARK
RAILINGS
HOLDING SPRIG OF BROOM

MALE GRIFFIN
GORGED WITH COGWHEELS
HOLDING LEAD MINER'S PICK
(COUNTY AND INDUSTRY)

*(CITY AND
ENVIRONMENT)*

STAG'S
HEADS

CHARLES
AND
HENRY
CAVENDISH
FRS

DIOCESE OF
LICHFIELD

DIOCESE OF
SOUTHWELL

ARMILLARY SPHERE
JOSEPH WRIGHT
AND
JOHN FLAMSTEED FRS

"EXPERIENCE TEACHES"
MOTTO OF DERBY COLLEGE
OF SCIENCE

The University of Derby
coat of arms:
'I designed this with
the very considerable
help of Malcolm Stirk,
and then negotiated the
final details with the
Richmond Herald at the
College of Arms.'
SOURCE: JONATHAN POWERS

Being left behind in the expansion of Higher Education, Derby was haemorrhaging young people. In 1989, the college was energised by new criteria for polytechnic status. The governing body was revamped with local professionals and businesspeople, and Alan Woods became chairman. Roger Waterhouse, a national pioneer of modular degrees and international exchange, was appointed as director. There were only 1,800 full-time and 2,400 part-time students (mostly at sub-degree level); just 7 first degrees, 3 masters programmes, and 13 research students.

When I first came here, as an external assessor for the CNAA, I was astonished. The morale, commitment, and clarity of purpose made the college feel like a coiled spring. Then the job of academic director was advertised. The two-day interview process gave everyone the chance to size up the candidates. Talk about hitting the ground running – the job had started the moment I had set foot on campus.

Yogita Yani, the 10,000th enrollee of 1993, the first time that annual enrolment reached a five-figure total.
SOURCE: JONATHAN POWERS

Ken Clarke's bombshell arrived just days after we had qualified to become a polytechnic. Failure now would put development into reverse, but no polytechnic had achieved what he demanded in less than a decade. In changing times you take your chances. Working at breakneck speed we created an impressive case to show we were in fact better prepared than some polytechnics. Needing a convincing way around the old rules, I recruited a highly distinguished Research Advisory Council as our guarantor. It was a close call at the final meeting of the CNAA, but we prevailed. The effect on recruitment of both staff and students was staggering – and most of the other colleges beat a path to my door. Michael Hall (later Deputy Vice-Chancellor) constructed new halls of residence, and deployed the insurance money to construct a huge technology building. We pioneered the first university bus service, and the first all-electronic enrolment process.

We also laid claim to tradition. In my 'spare time' I took on the decorative arrangements – official robes, academic dress, and the coat of arms. In 1977 the Ven. Richard Ninis had boldly driven through the merger of Bishop Lonsdale College with the Derby and District Colleges of Art and Technology. The independent but unincorporated trust ran on the unlimited personal liability of those in charge. In 1995 we became a limited company, with court members liable for just £1. Naturally, when the first *Times* league table appeared we came bottom — but we were on the list! Later I published an alternative table, dividing added value by unit cost — Derby then came top.

When I retired we had a worldwide operation of 25,000 students, burgeoning postgraduate and research activity, and millions of pounds of new buildings. Thanks to Roger's inspirational leadership, and the drive of his successor, John Coyne, with Hari Punchinhewa and their team, Kathryn Mitchell now leads a university with a bright future. We have been ranked in the top 50, and 6th relative to our former peer group. On the things Derby defines as important we are a regional leader. I enjoy enormous satisfaction from the achievements of the people I worked with and those who followed us.

The 14th Astronomer Royal, Sir Arnold Wolfendale FRS, posing with Lady Wolfendale, local historian Maxwell Craven, Professor Jonathan Powers, and Anthony Southwell, Chairman of Derby and District Astronomical Society, around a working orrery in front of Joseph Wright's famous painting, 1996.

SOURCE: JONATHAN POWERS

The University of Derby in 2017

Professor Kathryn Mitchell, Vice-Chancellor, University of Derby

The Vice-Chancellor of
the University of Derby,
Professor Kath Mitchell.
SOURCE: © RICHARD J.
RICHARDS

I JOINED the University of Derby as Vice-Chancellor in September 2015, having previously worked in academic institutions in London, Chicago, New York and Basel. So what brought me to Derby? The main factor for me was the university and the values it holds to providing high quality education within a city with a strong heritage for investment and innovation. Derby is a place with huge prospects; it has

a history of invention and making, is the home to several world-leading businesses, and has a thriving cultural scene, but at the heart of it are inspiring individuals that want to make Derby a vibrant community.

I was immediately struck by how committed everyone is to working together to continue to make the city an interesting and exciting place where people want to visit, live, work and study. I wanted to be part of that; I want the university to play a significant role in making this happen, so having the chance to become Vice-Chancellor was an opportunity I could not turn down.

The University of Derby is a community-based organisation and we want to help our local community. I have a passion for improving social mobility and seeing lives transformed through education, and these are areas in which I believe can help make a difference.

Our ambition is to provide our students with the best possible start in their careers through excellent teaching, delivered in cutting-edge facilities by staff who are experts in their field. We are also pleased to be recognised as a top 50 UK university (*Guardian*, 2017) and a top 20 UK university for teaching quality (*The Times*, 2017).

From humble beginnings the University of Derby has grown considerably in size and stature. Today, we have around 27,000 students including courses from apprenticeships to postgraduate research. In the last 10 years we have invested around £150 million in our campuses in Derby, Buxton, Leek and Chesterfield to make sure that our students have access to some of the best facilities in the UK. As part of this on-going improvement plan, we recently unveiled a £10.8 million sports centre, a custom-built forensic training facility and a £20 million home for Derby Law School.

University of Derby Sports Centre at the Kedleston Road campus with the main university buildings visible in the background. *The Derby Yearbook* was conceived, commissioned, designed, edited and typeset in East Tower by students on the first ever cohort of the MA Publishing that began in September 2016.

SOURCE: © ALISON LOYDALL

We work closely with the local business community to help them innovate, which in turn helps drive economic growth and improve the lives of people in the wider community. Research is at the heart of our university; from cutting the cost of cancer treatments to creating more accurate predictions of climate change, research is something that we take seriously. In fact, in 2014 three-quarters of our research output was judged to be internationally significant.

Another pioneering area of our provision is the University of Derby Online (UDOL). This provides online distance learning opportunities for students requiring a more flexible way of studying. From its inception in 2001, UDOL has grown considerably and we now have more than 3,000 students from over 100 countries studying with us.

Investing in the community is something that we are passionate about. In 2009 we bought and re-opened Derby Theatre (formerly the Derby Playhouse). Theatre is often the heartbeat of a city centre and our theatre has a long history of providing high quality drama. Also, it is now a 'learning theatre' funded with the support of the Arts Council that combines an exciting range of courses for students with a professional programme for the general public to enjoy as well as providing high quality productions.

Our Community Fund is another way in which we hope to give back to local people. Through this scheme, we award small grants to inspiring community

The main university campus at Kedleston Road.
SOURCE: © RICHARD J. RICHARDS

projects. Over the past two years the university has afforded £20,000 in grants to inspire projects that seek to benefit our communities in some way; including sports clubs, youth groups and small charities. Many of our students get involved in these local projects as well as through fundraising initiatives through the Students' Union RAG (Raise and Give) group.

Derby sits on the border of the Peak District, one of the best-loved National Parks in the country and one that I enjoy spending time exploring. We are particularly conscious of our responsibility towards the environment; installation of solar panels and wind turbines in our Derby campus has reduced our carbon footprint, but our ambition is to keep making improvements to reduce negative impact on our environment.

I feel incredibly privileged to work as the Vice-Chancellor of the University of Derby. Leading one of Derbyshire's largest employers that contributes around £560 million to the economy each year comes with a great deal of responsibility, but I am excited about what the future holds for the university and the city of Derby. As the city celebrates its fortieth anniversary, I think we have good cause to be optimistic. Derby really is an amazing and exciting place to live, work and study.

The main buildings at the Kedleston Road site are on pleasantly elevated ground. Unlike many campuses that sprawl widely, the University of Derby's main campus is compact, with teaching facilities, library and students' union all under one roof.

SOURCE © SALLY EDWARDS

Derby Book Festival

Jenny Denton and Sian Hoyle, Founders, Derby Book Festival

DERBY BOOK FESTIVAL was held for the first time in 2015. Although there had previously been several Festivals of Words, it was the first book-based festival to be held in the city for a number of years.

The festival, born over a glass of wine in QUAD, Derby's visual arts centre, was our brainchild. We are both keen readers and members of local book clubs, and we decided that a book festival was something that was missing from the city's cultural life. Jenny has previously worked in community development and corporate social responsibility and Sian's background was in marketing and events management. Armed with what we thought was an exciting idea, plenty of enthusiasm, and a few contacts, we started talking to the key arts organisations in the city. Without exception, the idea was met with support from all potential partners who recognised the benefits of a book festival to the city and to their own organisations. The University of Derby has been a significant supporter from the outset.

The Derby Book Festival launch, 2015. From left to right, Jenny, chair Liz Fothergill CBE, and Sian.
SOURCE: © BONBON PHOTOGRAPHY

The first Derby Book Festival was held 1–9 June 2015. The festival's vision was to create a city where residents value the unique ways in which books enrich their lives. Its aim was to bring Derby's residents together in a love of books and to inspire new readers to appreciate the pleasure and power of reading. From the beginning, the festival was to be rooted in the local community to demonstrate a sense of place. Not only did it aim to include events of local interest but also to organise related community projects to extend its reach into Derby's new communities.

The festival celebrates the joy of books and reading for all ages and interests. The programme includes a broad range of book-related events and activities, featuring internationally celebrated best-selling authors and poets. Authors appearing at the festivals have included Michael Morpurgo, Sebastian Faulks, Simon Armitage, Carol Ann Duffy, Tracy Chevalier, Sarah Waters, Louis de Bernières, Sunjeev Sahota, and David Nicholls, as well as a broad range of local writing talent.

The children's educational programme is a key element of the Festival. Each year, every Derby City primary school is invited to bring a group of children to a Meet the Author event in Derby Theatre. To date, authors have included Michael Morpurgo, Lauren Child, Marcia Williams, Andy Mulligan, Philip Reeve and Sarah McIntyre. Secondary schools have also been invited to host author visits and attend Meet the Author events. The Festival also includes an exciting children and families programme aimed at making reading and books fun with activities including street theatre, storytelling, illustrating, crafts, book stalls, quizzes, and competitions.

Artsbeat

Amanda Penman, Publishing Editor, Artsbeat

Derby is fast becoming the cultural heart of our county as the community puts the arts at the centre of everyday life. All over the city there are dedicated groups staging plays; writing novels, poetry, and music; painting; singing; and dancing. *Artsbeat* magazine strives to promote all this and more – in a free magazine available to everyone.

I have more than thirty years' experience as an editor and writer and four years ago decided to leave newspapers to create an independent monthly arts magazine for Derbyshire, to give a voice to the creatives who want to share their work with a wider audience. I knew that there was an awful lot going on in the community that many of us never heard about and I wanted to change that by providing a magazine for the arts. I had the skills to write, design, and distribute it, so I just thought I would give it a go and see what happened.

Although I was convinced there was enough going on to fill the pages every month I have been amazed at the response to *Artsbeat*. My email inbox is continually filling up with requests from organisations wanting to be included and I am never short of inspiration for features. The magazine would not exist at all if it were not for the support of organisations and businesses in the county who recognise the large audience it has and advertise with me or kindly act as a pick-up point for readers. It really is a magazine created for the community, by the community.

Cover of the February 2017 issue.

SOURCE: © ARTSBEAT

FORMAT Festival

Sohila Ayman, Assistant Editor, The Derby Yearbook

FORMAT festival has established a name for itself in the photography and media scene of the United Kingdom. Their programmes shed light on the art of photography and diverse media platforms such as documentaries, conceptual art, and other innovative projects. In today's world, photography and media are not only forms of expression, but are tools that help raise awareness of many causes. The festival relays the importance of imagery in creating dialogues between richly diverse cultures and backgrounds. FORMAT presents a range of exhibitions, discussion panels, and master classes amongst other events. It is organised by QUAD and the University of Derby, and is also supported by Arts Council England along with Derby City Council and several home and international partners.

Photograph from an event that was part of Derby Festé (see page 78).
SOURCE: SHARON STEVENS-CASH

Derby Festé

Sharon Stevens-Cash, Marketing Director, Derby Festé

DERBY FESTÉ is a cultural and colourful festival that takes place in Derby city centre every September. The event offers world-class entertainment and great food for people of all ages, attracting families, couples, and groups of friends. The streets come alive for two days with performers from all over the world – and some from closer to home. Since Festé landed in 2007 the event has seen audiences grow to 35,000 over the weekend.

Aerial performance outside QUAD.

Muaré – Voalá Company at Derby Festé, 2014.

Festé audience captivated
by a lantern show.
SOURCE: SHARON
STEVENS·CASH © STEVE
EGGLETON

A local resident calmly
takes a photograph of
a terrifying monster
outside Eagle Market.
SOURCE: SHARON
STEVENS·CASH © KEV RYAN

Derby Folk Festival

Bob Rushton, Co-Director, Derby Folk Festival

S TARTING LIFE in October 2007, the festival was originally called Derby Traditional Music and Arts Festival, to reflect the mix of music, dance, theatre, and craft traditions that were represented within it. Concerts and performances took place within the Assembly Rooms and Guildhall Theatre over a Friday evening and a full Saturday. It featured artists such as The Demon Barbers, Waterson:Carthy, John Tams, and Barry Coope. John Tams' appearance in the first year was coupled with him becoming the festival's founding patron, and he has been a great supporter of the event ever since. The festival was curated as a co-production between the Assembly Rooms and PR Promotions, with help from Derby City Council's enter-tainments department that became known as Derby LIVE in 2008.

Expanding to include Sunday events, the festival continued in a similar format until 2010, seeing headline performances from such names as Bellowhead, Eliza Carthy, Edward II, Shooglenifty, and Oysterband. In 2011, the festival simplified its name, changing to Derby Folk Festival. Events continued through Derby LIVE's indoor venues, with the festival gathering critical acclaim for a great atmosphere, and headliners including Show of Hands, Home Service, Peatbog Faeries, and Seth Lakeman.

In 2013, Lucy Ward joined John Tams as festival patron, and fringe events began to be arranged, including free music on the Market Place. After a plant room fire closed the Assembly Rooms in March 2014, the move outside took on an even greater significance as the main concerts for 2014 took place inside a large marquee that covered the Market Place. The festival also found great support from the recently renovated Old Bell Hotel, which opened its doors to the ballroom early, in order to help with festival space. Media attention from the Assembly Rooms' fire, and great headline acts in the shape of Steeleye Span, Show of Hands, and Kate Rusby saw the festival sell out.

The presence of the festival on the Market Place brought the event to the heart of the city, further increasing its significance for audiences and city-based businesses alike. In 2015, to expand the number of concerts, Derby Cathedral was added to

Band playing at Derby Folk Festival.

SOURCE: BOB RUSHTON © GRAHAM WHITMORE

the festival. Since the first festival, the city's streets have been brightened by the sight and sound of traditional dance sides who provide entertainment, whilst raising awareness of the festival.

Celebrating ten years of festivals in 2016, audiences continue to visit from afar. Festival artists always include major names on the folk circuit, along with new and emerging talent, and thanks to the abundance of top class artists hailing from Derbyshire, the locality is well represented at all levels.

Classical Music

Mike Wheeler, Freelance Writer; Adult Education Tutor, WEA

S INCE 1996 Derby has been home to Sinfonia Viva, a professional chamber orchestra that celebrates its 35th anniversary in 2017. Duncan Ward has been Principal Conductor since 2015. The orchestra presents concerts and educational events in the city and throughout the East Midlands. With the Assembly Rooms currently out of action, its main Derby performance base is the Cathedral, where it gives both full-length evening concerts and shorter performances in the early evenings. Each year the orchestra works with local schoolchildren and students on a series of themed workshops, culminating in a performance at Derby Theatre.

Derby Chamber Music, founded in 1997, promotes an annual series of professional chamber music recitals at the University of Derby's Multi-Faith Centre, by a mixture of well-known musicians and up-and-coming younger performers, in an eight-concert season running from October to April.

Derby's amateur classical music organisations include two choral societies, Derby Bach Choir, conducted by Richard Roddis, and Derby Choral Union, conducted by Richard Dacey – founded in 1866, this is one of the oldest choral societies in the United Kingdom. Smaller choirs include the Derwent Singers, conducted by Richard Roddis, and the Sitwell Singers, conducted by Malcolm Goldring. Derby Concert Orchestra, conducted by Jonathan Trout, gives five concerts a year in the Cathedral – including its popular Christmas concert – St Peter's Church, Littleover; and St Mary's Church, Wirksworth.

Derby Cathedral Choir, with boy and girl trebles, works alongside the all-adult, mixed voice Cathedral Voluntary Choir. As well as singing for services, both choirs give occasional concerts. The all-adult Derby Choristers are also based at the Cathedral. The Cathedral promotes a series of organ recitals on Wednesdays in July and August every year.

The VoiceBox, a converted former industrial building near the city centre, is a teaching, rehearsal, and performance venue for a range of vocal and choral music. It is also host to a number of outside organisations, including Derby Music Club, which promotes concerts arranged and performed by its members, and Kaleidoscope Community Choir.

From Playhouse to Theatre

Emeritus Professor Jonathan Powers DL Hon DUniv

T HE new Derby Playhouse opened in 1975 – a huge undertaking made possible by a commercial loan to cover the shortfall of an appeal. The Duke of Devonshire opened the theatre, which enjoyed an official visit from Princess Alexandra. That season, Alan Bates headed a stellar cast for Chekhov's *The Seagull*. Roderick Ham's design was a far cry from the original Little Theatre with its postage stamp stage. With wings doubling the size of the stage, a fly-tower, hydraulic thrust-stage, sub-stage, bridges, 'slots' off hidden stairs, and workshops, it was a veritable theatrical engine.

The Playhouse, photographed in 1975.
SOURCE: JONATHAN POWERS

HRH Princess Alexandra
signing the special
visitors' book in the
presence of Major Malin
on 28 November 1975.
SOURCE: JONATHAN POWERS

I joined the board in 1995, hoping to forge university links, for I knew how theatre students enhance a campus. Derby Playhouse was thriving under Artistic Director, Mark Clements, and its dedicated Chief Executive, David Edwards. The Chairman, Denis Barlow, had plans to expand but suddenly died. Sue Haskew took over and I became her vice-chairman.

Derby had the region's smallest professional auditorium and the lowest funding per seat, but a very loyal audience. Mark's Godber comedies, musicals, and pantomimes packed the theatre. *Cinderella's* flying horse took our breath away. Corin Redgrave gave a masterclass in *The Browning Version*. Andrew Bovell's *Speaking with Tongues* was stunning – a quartet for voices where two scenes play simultaneously. In 1999 we were acclaimed the Most Welcoming Theatre in England. But underfunding threatened the future. In

2002 Karen Hebden and Stephen Edwards became chief executive and creative producer – doubling as outstanding artistic directors and playwrights.

Audiences rose above 100,000. Most plays got national reviews – three-quarters with four or five stars. We won the Civic Society Award for the Best Refurbishment of 2003. At the Arts and Business Awards in 2004, our Egg Academy not only won the Community Award, but was declared overall champion for the Most Inspiring and Beneficial Partnership in the whole of the UK. In 2005 our Hot Tickets Scheme, and the Community Theatre, were both shortlisted, and the City Partnership awarded us the accolade of Outstanding Ambassador for Derby. Three shows were shortlisted for national theatrical awards, including Stephen's *Moon Landing*.

I handed over to Michael Hall to take forward plans for a new three-auditorium theatre. But this collapsed when the City Council withdrew. Things were set for long-term success until the impact of the building work for the new shopping centre. But when it opened, audiences soared to record levels. Michael Hall resigned when the principal funders refused to advance grant instalments to avert a crisis. But the theatre never ran out of money, despite spending over £30,000 on professional

Programme for *The Irresistible Rise of Arturo Ui* by Dario Fo, directed by Chris Honer in 1983.
SOURCE: JONATHAN POWERS

The staff on stage with Annie Castledine, front row fourth from left, uncorking a bottle of champagne at the fortieth anniversary of the Little Theatre, 1988.
SOURCE: JONATHAN POWERS

FROM PLAYHOUSE TO THEATRE

advice. However, at 3:15 p.m. on Thursday 29 November 2007, the Playhouse was declared closed. The staff refused to leave and the liquidators joined the audience! The BBC filmed the occasion. Thanks to the upsurge of public support we reopened a week later. *The Guardian*'s review gave *Treasure Island* five stars: 'a show too good to miss in a theatre too valuable to lose'. Having chaired the Rescue Consortium, I returned to chair a new board.

Despite the theatre operating successfully, the principal funders both refused to provide support. There was a protracted rescue struggle. The global financial crash undermined our first attempt. It seemed the best solution was for the university to acquire the theatre. The major creditors supported us. Thanks to Stephen and Karen's extraordinary commitment, Derby still has a professional theatre. Derby Theatre has become a resurgent theatrical force, providing a new model. Under the brilliant direction of Sarah Brigham, her staff old and new, and with students of theatre arts, the spirit of Derby Playhouse lives on, in a theatre with a bright future.

Flying horse and carriage designed by Alan Jackson in a production of *Cinderella*, 2000. The Playhouse sold it on for £15,000. 'It only lasted ninety seconds, but no-one who saw it will have forgotten'.
SOURCE: JONATHAN POWERS

Derby Hippodrome Theatre

Joan Travis, Chair, Derby Hippodrome Restoration Trust

L IKE Marmite, the old Hippodrome theatre seems to divide Derbeians' opinions; there are those who look at the damage that has been done to it recently and say that it should be knocked down, and those who know its history, see that it could play an important role in the future, and think it should be restored. The theatre, designed by Marshall & Tweedy, was opened in July 1914, with stalls, two circles, and a capacity of 2,000. As well as being a variety theatre, it had a unique bioscope, affording the ability to show films along with live shows. It was converted to a cinema in 1930. From 1950 to 1959 there were only live shows, until it became a bingo hall. As with many theatres, the bingo ensured the upkeep of the building until 2007, when it was sold to the present owner.

In 2013, the Derby Hippodrome Restoration Trust successfully applied for the Hippodrome to be the first theatre in the country to be registered as a Community Asset. The Trust had a planning application approved in 2014 to do restoration work on the theatre, including installing a protective roof. However, purchasing the building is proving more difficult as the owners do not wish to sell.

Derby has to decide whether it would be good to have a large theatre, like Sheffield, Nottingham, Leicester, and Stoke. These cities have at least two theatres, and would argue that theatre space allows for many cultural activities to flourish. In turn, this brings in considerable revenue for these cities, as well as innumerable benefits for people in terms of enjoyment, education, and general wellbeing. To be fair, many people in Derby have spoken in favour of having a new theatre since the Assembly Rooms were closed. Derby Theatre, situated in the Intu centre, run by the University, who thankfully rescued it after it was closed, is doing a sterling job. However, the seating capacity is low in comparison to that available in our nearest cities, and an extra, larger space would benefit Derby. Hence, there have been proposals for a new building. The costs would inevitably be upwards of £80 million, a figure unlikely to be allocated. Those who once enjoyed nights out in the beautifully decorated green and gold Hippodrome theatre, and also the next generation, the grandchildren of the former, and newly arrived students, would love to see such a theatre restored as a part of modern Derby.

The original ceiling
and proscenium of the
Hippodrome Theatre.

Seeing it today, in its dreadful state after the arson attacks, a stranger might assume that it was beyond repair, but no. The Hippodrome Restoration Trust has commissioned professionals to assess the structure, and, in a nutshell, it is a half-constructed theatre. Foundations still exist on the site, and it could be renewed in a third of the time and at a third of the cost, in comparison to a new build. Once restored, the Hippodrome would contribute considerably to the cultural life of the city. It would lead to the regeneration of the Green Lane area, a formerly attractive and important part of Derby. It will be interesting to see which way the people of Derby will vote.

Derby LIVE

Dr Pete Meakin, Creative Producer, Derby LIVE

THE Guildhall was built in 1828 as Derby's Town Hall. Following a fire in 1841, a state visit by Queen Victoria in 1891, and the infamous trial of Alice Wheeldon in 1917, it closed in 1949 with the opening of the new Council House on Corporation Street. The council then converted the building into a theatre, which opened in 1975. The Guildhall Theatre is a Grade II listed building. It is a small and intimate venue that is predominantly used by amateur theatre groups and dance schools, in addition to hosting folk, comedy, children's entertainment, jazz, and touring theatre events. There are large and small clubrooms located adjacent to the venue, which are used for 'fringe-type' performances, small exhibitions, rehearsals, educational workshops, trade shows, and CD and book fairs.

Gig in the Assembly Rooms great hall.
SOURCE: DERBY LIVE
© GRAHAM WHITMORE

The Grade II listed
Guildhall cast in
autumnal shades.
SOURCE: DERBY LIVE

The original Assembly Rooms was built between 1765 and 1774, but it was destroyed by a fire in 1963. The new Assembly Rooms was opened in 1977 by the Queen Mother. On 14 March 2014, the building again suffered a fire in the plant room above the adjoining car park. The fire destroyed the plant room and made the Assembly Rooms unusable.

Having previously operated as the Assembly Rooms and Guildhall Theatre, in February 2008 Derby LIVE was created, also encompassing Derby City Council's programme of major outdoor events and festivals. This programme included such long-established favourites as: The Darley Park Concert, the Markeaton Park Bonfire and Fireworks Display, and the Christmas Lights Switch-On. Since then, Derby LIVE has increased its portfolio of outdoor events and festivals which it produces and co-produces, including such annual highlights as Derby Festé and the St George's Day celebrations. Derby LIVE also continues to support a wide range of events and festivals across the city produced by other leading partners such as the Caribbean Carnival, the summer Beer Festival, and The Big One at Chaddesden Park.

Between 2009 and 2012, while also managing the main house of Derby Theatre (formerly Derby Playhouse) in a unique partnership with the University of Derby,

The original Assembly Rooms were built between 1765 and 1774. This new Assembly Rooms opened in 1997.

SOURCE: DERBY LIVE

Derby LIVE held the lead responsibility in the city for professional, locally produced theatre. Highlights of this period include: *Onassis* starring Robert Lindsay, which transferred to the West End; Director of Derby LIVE Peter Ireson's winning of the TMA Theatre Manager of the Year Award in 2010; and *The Go-Between*, winner of the 2012 TMA Award for Best Musical and which also transferred to the West End. During this period, Derby LIVE delivered 31 new productions, 18 of which were world premieres, across a range of venues including Derby Theatre, Guildhall Theatre, Assembly Rooms' Darwin Suite, Cathedral Green, and site-specific work. Derby LIVE also provided the highest quality participatory theatre learning and performance opportunities through its Playmakers programme, its Youth Theatre, and its Community Theatre.

Fireworks watched by a sizeable crowd, 2015.

QUAD

Jessica Saunders, Marketing Officer, QUAD

QUAD, which opened on the Market Place in September 2008, is Derby's centre for art and film, with an independent cinema, contemporary art gallery, vibrant café bar, and digital resources open to everyone.

QUAD was created when two well-established arts organisations from Derby – Q Arts and Metro Cinema – joined forces with Derby City Council to create a cultural partnership. The experience of the former organisations and QUAD's purpose-built building have reinforced Derby's growing reputation on the national cultural scene, attracting some of the most significant and important names in the world of art and film to the city through the varied programme of exhibitions, films, events, and festivals. Our original patron was the late, great Sir John Hurt CBE, and current patrons include musician John Tams and actors Jack O'Connell and Paddy

Cinema One event at QUAD.

SOURCE: QUAD © GRAHAM LUCAS COMMONS

QUAD, on the Market
Place in the Cathedral
Quarter.

Considine. QUAD is a registered independent charity that receives funding to support its charitable aims from a variety of sources including Derby City Council and Arts Council England. This money is used to create and support our free exhibitions, education, and creative wellbeing programmes which include regular groups such as Listen Love Learn (for parents with children under 5), GoldsQUAD (for people over 50), and Q Club (for children on the autistic spectrum or with additional needs).

All profits from commercial activities, including cinema ticket sales and café bar sales, are reinvested in the programme and infra-structure of QUAD allowing us to continue to innovate and inspire on a local, national, and international level. Our activities generate millions for Derby's economy as well as positive international media coverage. QUAD does not have shareholders, profit share schemes, or regular annual wage increases; QUAD exists to make art and film acces-sible to all, to improve the cultural life of the city, and to celebrate Derby to the world.

Déda

Stephen Munn, Artistic Director and CEO, Déda

Déda was established as local dance development agency, Derby Dance, in 1991. Initially based at Derby Playhouse, it became one of the first waves of National Lottery funded capital projects and moved to its current premises on Chapel Street in 1997. In August 2008, after rebranding, the organisation changed its name to Déda, a blend of its former title, to reflect the broader scope of its work and ambitions to fulfil Derby's evolving cultural needs. Déda's mission is to deliver an exceptional programme of dance, contemporary circus, and outdoor performance to as wide an audience as possible, and to be recognised for its outstanding contribution in the field of dance development and learning. By providing a ladder of creative opportunities for artists, audiences, and participants, Déda aims to foster an understanding of, and respect for, dance and related art forms.

Déda, on Chapel Street, was established in 1991.
SOURCE: DÉDA

Leviathan, presented by
James Wilton Dance.
SOURCE: DÉDA © STEVE
TANNER

In 2014 Déda redeveloped part of Queen's Leisure Centre, expanding its facilities to include a new state of the art studio and production space with aerial rig, and improving its meeting and conference room spaces. The Déda theatre was also dramatically improved to enable the presentation of larger scale productions – both by in-house youth performance companies and national visiting companies. Déda houses a 124-capacity studio theatre, three dance studios, meeting room facilities, and the CUBE café and bar. It offers a weekly class programme and a year-round professional performance programme for children, young people, and adults, as well as an extensive community development programme. Déda enriches the lives of 55,000 people annually, offering an inspiring programme of performance, production, and participation through a balance of work that is both accessible and challenging. Déda's academy programme alone engages with over 13,000 children and young people a year whilst sister company Déda Producing, artistic lead for international outdoor arts festival Festé, reaches an annual audience of 35,000 across the city.

In addition, Déda has developed strong partnerships within the city, strengthened with the recent addition of a Bachelor of Arts Degree in Dance delivered in partnership with University of Derby and by becoming a key part of Derby's health and education commissioning network. Working with national and international artists, Déda is also at the forefront of talent development in the region, supporting resident companies and exciting young talent. Déda is proud to be continually growing, changing, and evolving with the city, enhancing the Midlands' cultural offering, and continually striving to achieve its overall vision: to enrich people's lives through dance and the arts.

Derbyshire County Cricket Club

Jordan Reynolds, Assistant Editor, The Derby Yearbook

D ERBYSHIRE County Cricket Club was founded in November 1870 after a three-year campaign led by club secretary Walter Bowden. The first president of the club was the 7th Earl of Chesterfield, who had played for and against All-England. The club is one of 18 first-class county clubs which make up the England and Wales domestic cricket structure.

The Racecourse Ground, originally home of Derby County Football Club, now to Derbyshire CCC. SOURCE: © ALISON LOYDALL.

Derbyshire's first captain was Samuel Richardson, a gentleman's tailor, who led the team to its first victories. Supporting the team with his incredible bowling strength was seasoned professional Dove Gregory, who had been playing for a cricket team since the 1850s. Also making their debut were amateurs such as Robert Smith, John Smith, and John Burnham; a farmer, solicitor, and clerk respectively. Derbyshire's first match, one of two matches they played that year, was in May 1871 against Lancashire at Old Trafford, where Derbyshire fast bowler, Dove Gregory, tore apart Lancashire's batsmen. Derbyshire went on to win this first match by innings and eleven runs, setting a precedent for the team to follow. Lancashire replied in August of the same year by winning against Derbyshire by 62 runs.

The years after 1871 were turbulent for Derbyshire County Cricket Club and in 1888, after suffering several significant losses, they were demoted from first-class status. Derbyshire, however, were determined to regain their position. After several hard-fought matches in 1893 – that culminated

The main stand at Derbyshire County Cricket Club's ground.

in wins against teams such as Essex, Leicestershire, and Hampshire – Derbyshire regained their first-class status and have held on to it since. It was not until 1936, after their 38th season in the county championship, that Derbyshire finally won the competition for the first and only time. Derbyshire County Cricket Club remains a strong team to this day, having recently won the County Championship 2nd division title in 2012 under the captaincy of Wayne Madsen.

Derby County Football Club

Connor Brown, Editor, The Derby Yearbook

DERBY COUNTY Football Club was established in 1884 as a splinter from Derbyshire County Cricket Club so that players would have something to do during the winter. Their nickname, The Rams, derives from the clubs association with the First Regiment of Derby Militia, whose own mascot was a ram. Sometime in the 1890s Derby adopted its famous black and white strip, with earlier kits having been amber, brown, and light blue.

The Rams shared their first stadium with the cricket club but moved to the Baseball Ground in 1895. It was during Derby's time here that a curse was supposedly placed on the club because they had evicted a group of travellers from the premises. Allegedly, the curse would ensure that The Rams never won the FA Cup. The team reached six FA Cup semi-finals between 1896 and 1903 and reached the final three times, but they never won. It was 43 years before Derby reached another final, where it is believed that a member of the club met with the traveller community to have the curse lifted. As they were tied 1–1 with Charlton Athletic, the ball burst, and this was proclaimed as the moment that the curse was broken. Derby won the match 4–1. Some say that it was Jackie Stamps who paid to have the curse lifted. Stamps went on to score twice.

A view of The Gordon Guthrie Stand, Pride Park Stadium. Gordon Guthrie was DCFC's longest-serving member of staff, spending over sixty years with the club.
SOURCE: © ALISON LOYDALL

Brian Clough and Peter Taylor took over the club in 1967. The Rams were promoted to the First Division in 1969, finished fourth in 1970, won the league in 1972, and the following year reached the semi-finals of the European Cup, where they lost to Juventus. There is a statue of Clough and Taylor standing proud outside Pride Park. Since 1997 this has been the club's home, costing around £28 million to build. Through a £7 million ten-year deal the ground was named the iPro Stadium, but the contract was cut short, with the club reverting to the name Pride Park in 2017. Pride Park has a capacity of 33,597, making it the 16th largest football ground in England. This pales in comparison to Derby's record attendance of 41,826 at a game at the Baseball Stadium in 1969, where Derby beat Tottenham Hotspur 5–0. Derby County FC is renowned for its loyal fan base and for achieving high attendance year on year.

Statue of Brian Clough
and Peter Taylor by
Andy Edwards, 2010.
SOURCE: © ALISON LOYDALL

Ye Olde Dolphin Inne

James Harris, Landlord, Ye Olde Dolphin Inne

Y E OLDE DOLPHIN INNE is Derby's oldest pub, dating back to 1530, and I have been the landlord for 14 years. The pub is steeped in history and has several resident ghosts, one that I have actually seen for myself. I was working in one of the upstairs rooms, I looked up and saw the back end of a Victorian-style dress go through the wall in front of me. This is supposedly The Grey Lady, only ever seen by a handful of licensees at the pub. The cellar of the pub was used as a mortuary many years ago, making use of the naturally cold environment. There is an infamous story that there was a young lady who was hanged in the marketplace. Her body was brought back to Ye Olde Dolphin Inne and dropped into the cellar. Allegedly there was a doctor who started doing an autopsy on the young woman when he found that she was still alive. Her tortured soul still haunts the cellar to this day. These are just a couple of stories that surround this wonderful pub. My wife Josephine and I are very proud to be custodians of Derby's oldest pub, and perhaps one day somebody will be talking about our time here at the Dolphin in historical terms.

Ye Olde Dolphin Inne on Queen Street dates back to 1530.
SOURCE: © CARNEGIE

Eagle Market, Boxing, and Wrestling

Francis 'Frank' Woodhouse, Market Trader, Eagle Market

M Y GRANDAD was Frank, my dad was Frank, and I am Francis Woodhouse, also known as Frank: three generations of market traders. I own a pet shop and greengrocers' in Eagle Market. There used to be sixty fruit and vegetable stalls, and now there are three. It is well-known that supermarkets damaged market traders' business, but just when the damage seemed to have been done even cheaper supermarkets appeared, the likes of Aldi and Lidl.

Big Daddy and an unidentified wrestler during a bout. Three generations of Woodhouse organised wrestling in Derby.

Playbill for the first
wrestling bouts at the
Assembly Rooms, 1977.

Playbill for wresting
bouts at Drill Hall, 1946.
SOURCE: © FRANCIS
WOODHOUSE

Cucumbers were not allowed to be grown during the war, but a plant nursery
owner at Castle Donington painted the windows of his greenhouse white, grew
them, and sold them on the black market to sandwich shops that were providing
salmon and cucumber sandwiches for ridiculous prices. My grandfather's van was
once parked outside the market when his wing mirror was pulled off by the trunk
of a passing elephant. Luckily one of the police officers saw the incident from the
top floor of the police station, otherwise I wonder whether my granddad would
have been believed.

Before the Second World War my granddad was the Midland's forces champion at his weight in boxing and started the Boxing Club in Derby's West End. He started promoting boxing in 1932 and he did this until war broke out. After the war, and due to the high fees demanded by the boxers, he turned to wrestling. The first wrestling show was at the Drill Hall, on Becket Street, on 23 September 1946. The success of the shows meant that it was moved to the King's Hall in January 1948. I knew who would win the shows; my granddad said that 'you shouldn't miss the fifth round of the second bout, it'll be great, but don't tell'. Lord Scarsdale once asked my grandad to stage a show in front of Kedleston Hall. The first bout was Alan Woods versus Melvyn Wriss who were both lightweights. It was fantastic. In 1972 and 1973 my granddad and dad died so my mum, my brother, and I carried it on. We had our first show in the Assembly Rooms on 14 November 1977 where Mick McManus and Shirley 'Big Daddy' Crabtree headlined. The last wrestling shows were in 1985 and unfortunately we have never started again.

Advertisement from a wresting programme for Frank Woodhouse & Son, greengrocers, 1984.

SOURCE: © FRANCIS WOODHOUSE

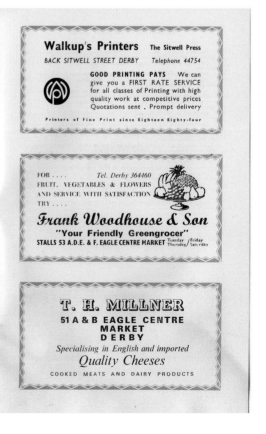

Intu Derby

Samantha Joanne Luton, Assistant Editor, The Derby Yearbook

O N 20 November 1975, Derby's iconic shopping centre was opened to the public after £7 million was invested in its development. Originally named the Eagle Centre, it was built on a site formerly occupied by several streets of terraced housing, all of which were demolished during construction. One of these, Eagle Street, was the inspiration behind its name. The shopping centre has undergone several renovations over the years, including a rebuild of the market in 1990 and a complete refurbishment in 1999. On 9 October 2007, television presenter Tess Daly opened a £340 million extension on the site of the former Castlefields Main Centre. The extension introduced one hundred new stores, including Debenhams

Eagle Market, where you will find numerous market stalls, including Francis Woodhouse's fruit and vegetable stall.
SOURCE: © ALISON LOYDALL

and Marks & Spencer, who both closed their high-street establishments, upgrading to the larger, centralised location of the shopping centre. It also contained an 800-seat eating zone and the £30 million 12-screen Showcase Cinema de Lux. The shopping centre was renamed Westfield Derby and on 1 May 2014 became Intu Derby, after being bought by Intu Properties. Intu Derby opened its £2.4 million ten-pin bowling alley, Hollywood Bowl, on 11 April 2017. Based on Level 3, its all-American themed venue includes a retro dining experience as well as four VIP lanes named after celebrity icons Marilyn Monroe, Han Solo, Audrey Hepburn, and Elvis Presley.

Eagle Market adjoins the shopping centre and is the United Kingdom's largest indoor market. Until 2007 it was known as the Eagle Centre Market and was considered part of the shopping centre alongside Derby Theatre, although operated by Derby City Council. However, after the Westfield Group and Hermès acquisition, the council dropped 'centre' rather than taking on the Westfield name, establishing it as an independent entity with separate branding.

Intu Derby dates back to 1975, and has since undergone a number of name changes and redevelopments.

Night Markets

Sheena Holland, Designer and Events Organiser, Night Markets

I AM an artist in Derby and have lived here for 14 years. My Night Market work in the city started when the independent shops in the Cathedral Quarter took a blow in footfall due to the opening of the Intu shopping centre. My shop at the time was in the Cathedral Quarter. I started a monthly market in Blacksmith's Yard on Sadler Gate to attract more customers. Sadler Gate was struggling; it had 12 empty shops, The Strand arcade had only two shops open, and Blacksmith's Yard had no tenants.

The Market started in March 2014 and attendance hit 3,500 on the first day, with 45 stalls present. November 2014 saw the first Night Market stem from the Sadler Gate markets with an attendance of 7,500 and 52 stall holders. Since 2014 we have hit footfall figures of 22,000 at our Christmas events, with 220 stall holders attending our one-night events. Our Night Markets came runner-up in Best Market 2016 in *The Guardian*, voted by readers.

The Night Market provides a platform for Derby's creative community of designers, artists, and makers to sell their wares. In the last four years the shops in the areas I use for the markets have become fully tenanted — there are no empty shops — which I feel has been helped somewhat by having regular footfall from the markets.

Pyclets

Bill Monk, Director, LOCS Limited

To me, as a youngster, pyclets were made in a ring on a hotplate, nowadays they are called crumpets. Flat pyclets were made from the same batter mix but without rings, today they are called pikelets or pyclets. My earliest recollections of the family business were from visits to my uncle's house on North Parade with my father, Jimmy Monk, who was a musician and band leader. He organised the music and bands at the Plaza Ballroom, the Trocadero, and other places. The

Emily Monk sold pyclets in Derby right up until her death.

family business predominantly made pyclets, oatcakes, and occasionally scones and bread. It was started in the early 1900s on Willow Row and then split in to separate businesses on Stanhope Street and North Parade, run respectively by brothers Ernest and William, my grandfather. William died before I was born and the North Parade business was continued by William's formidable widow, Emily, and her three sons, Tom, Jimmy, and Joe. The business was not profitable enough to support all the sons and their families, so Tom took over the day-to-day baking with his mother Emily running the stall in the Guildhall entrance. Jimmy and Joe went off to earn a living separately and to provide support to the family business.

The North Parade premises were interesting. The house had many rooms, a big shop, a separate workshop, stables, outbuildings, and a bake house: it was fascinating. There was a huge mixer with a long coke-fired hotplate stove capable of cooking about 120 pyclets at a time. There were two smaller gas fired hotplates which were quicker to heat up but could not produce the volume needed at weekends. The pyclet process consisted of laying out the rings on the stove, filling each one with batter, and then turning them over. When cooked, the pyclets in their rings were thrown in to a knocking-out tray to be cooled before the rings could be removed. Knocking-out was one of my Saturday pocket money jobs. The produce was then packed in wicker baskets and loaded on to a large handcart which was pushed to the Market Hall to be sold by Emily. Emily kept the stand going for over forty years; she walked to work every day stopping in the Cathedral to pray. She never retired and was there in all weathers.

Flat pyclets cooking in a pan: flat because, unlike crumpets, they are not cooked in rings.
SOURCE: © CLAIRE SUTTON IMAGES

St Peter's Quarter

Helen Wathall, Managing Director, G. Wathall and Son Limited

S T P ETER' S Quarter Business Improvement District was formed on 1 September 2011. The Business Improvement District was set up, run, and funded by businesses within the quarter through an agreed levy. As business representatives, we all give our time voluntarily, putting something back into the community we work in. The Business Improvement District is designed to tackle issues identified by the businesses in the area.

The diversity of St Peter's Quarter provides a varied environment aiming to complement the city's already established Intu Shopping Centre and the Cathedral Quarter. Stretching from Riverlights in the east, across to Macklin Street in the west, and from Osmaston Road in the south, to Victoria Street in the north, areas of improvement are continually identified alongside the promotion of our existing services; this improves the experience for visitors and the people of Derby alike.

St Peter's Quarter Business Improvement District can be proud of its achievements since 2011, and, as chair of the board, I am looking forward to building on this with our plan for 2017–22, which aims to deliver additional services to the district with a budget of £1 million. This includes our uniformed rangers, who welcome visitors and support businesses in dealing with antisocial behaviour. As the fifth generation of G. Wathall and Son Ltd, funeral directors on Macklin Street, I am proud to be a part of St Peter's Quarter Business Improvement District.

Parksafe car park on Bold Lane made headlines in 2004 when it was rated among the ten most secure locations worldwide, alongside Area 51 and the bank vault at Fort Knox.
SOURCE: © ALISON LOYDALL

Lara Croft

Elliot Ralph, Assistant Editor, The Derby Yearbook

OVER the past three decades gaming has come to house numerous iconic figures. Alongside Mario and Master Chief in the video game hall of fame sits a certain Derby-born legend: Lara Croft. Lara Croft was originally created by Toby Gard, a designer working at Core Design's Ashbourne Road office, as a female equivalent to Indiana Jones. After five redesigns, in 1996 Lara made her debut as the star of the first Tomb Raider game. Core Design's unique creation proved to be a critical and commercial success. Lara's first adventure was met with glowing praise and managed to sell 7.5 million copies. In the years that followed, the pixelated heroine cemented her position as one of the flagship mascots for Sony's original Playstation, with her name being used in promotional campaigns alongside Crash Bandicoot and Spyro. Lara's success also helped to put Derby on the video game map, as her success encouraged other developers to consider Derby as their creative home.

To date, the Tomb Raider gaming franchise is estimated to have sold 58 million copies. Lara has also delved into other forms of media, with two hit movies starring Angelina Jolie grossing over £345 million. In 2006, Lara entered the *Guinness Book of World Records* as the most successful videogame heroine. The city of Derby has also honoured Lara's legacy and took pride in being her home. In 2010, after receiving over 89 per cent of the tallied votes, Derby City Council announced that its citizens had voted to name the city's new ring road Lara Croft Way to commemorate the impact her creation has had on the city. Lara may now reside in Crystal Dynamic's California studio but her original home will always be Derby.

The Women's Institute

Christine Gardner, Trustee, Derbyshire Federation of Women's Institutes

THE HEAD OFFICE for the Derbyshire Federation of the WI has been in Derby since 1918. Firstly, we were in The Hostel on Full Street which was on the site of Erasmus Darwin's house. We then moved to Hefford's Building in 1926, and then on to St Mary's Chambers, both on Queens Street, in 1931. In 1935, the head office moved to Community House on Kedleston Road which is now part of Emmanuel School. Finally, in 1974 we purchased Derbyshire House with the money raised from our members' fundraising activities, and a grant received from Derbyshire County Council. A dedicated group of members, armed with brooms, buckets, paint, wallpaper, and scrapers, descended on the neglected premises and transformed a building that resembled something out of a Dickens novel to a bright, functioning head office in true WI fashion. Derbyshire Federation still owns the same building, although many improvements and refurbishments have taken place over the years. We are proud of our hall that provides a venue for many activities in the community and holds excellent events for WI members. The WI provides education and friendship and gets involved in many events held in the local community.

Acknowledgements

Connor Brown, Editor, The Derby Yearbook

A PROJECT such as this would not have been possible without the assistance of our enthusiastic contributors: thank you to all of you; your insights, gained through your personal experiences of this great city, have helped produce a book that is honest and wholesome in a way that it simply would not have been without the variety of people involved.

We are grateful to the talented Alison Loydall, who provided many of the photographs, as well as the contributors that allowed us to use their own illustrations. Thank you to Derby Museums Trust for allowing us to use a number of images from their wonderful collection, Carnegie Publishing for allowing us to use photographs from their book *Derbyshire: A History*, and Claire Sutton for allowing us to use her photograph of some pyclets. The Science & Society Picture Library were very helpful with all our enquiries. The source of each photograph is given in a credit line by the photograph in question. Luke Taplin-McCallum captured the spirit of the project in his wonderful cover design.

Our project was given considerable confirmation when the Duke of Devonshire agreed to write our foreword – thank you for lending your name to our work. Emeritus Professor Jonathan Powers was restless in connecting us with his network of contacts; the end result would have been a shadow of what it now is were it not for your help. Maxwell Craven provided insightful historical information that helped form various sections. Thank you Alistair Hodge for your guidance, and the University of Derby for your generous financial support.

Lauren Elizabeth Taylor helped with typesetting and Esmé Leaning with research. Thank you to Alison Loydall, David Barker, and Melissa Dennis for their help in promoting the book. I save my greatest thanks for my editorial team, without whom the project would have been unmanageable. Thank you to Amy Drew, Debbie Kruger, Elliot Ralph, Emily Eaton, Jessica Hutchby, Jordan Reynolds, Katy Mitchell, Samantha Joanne Luton, Shannon Colley, and Sohila Ayman for your support, advice, and hard work; your friendship was invaluable.

Contributors

Authors

Alex Rock, Development Officer, Derby Cathedral

Alistair Hodge, MA Publishing programme leader, University of Derby

Amanda Penman, Publishing Editor, Artsbeat

Amy Drew, Assistant Editor, The Derby Yearbook

Arran Paul Johnston, Director, Scottish Battlefields Trust

Bill Monk, Director, LOCS Limited

Bob Rushton, Co-Director, Derby Folk Festival

Christine Gardner, Trustee, Derbyshire Federation of Women's Institutes

Connor Brown, Editor, The Derby Yearbook

Elliot Ralph, Assistant Editor, The Derby Yearbook

Dr Hardial Singh Dhillon, Sikh Advisor to the University of Derby

Fran Wickes, Parish Catechetical Coordinator, St Mary's Church

Francis 'Frank' Woodhouse, Market Trader, Eagle Market

Helen Wathall, Managing Director, G. Wathall and Son Limited

Idris Sadat, Islamic Scholar, Minister of Religion

Jacqueline Smith, Curator, Royal Crown Derby Museum

James Harris, Landlord, Ye Olde Dolphin Inne

Jenny Denton, Founder, Derby Book Festival

Jessica Saunders, Marketing Officer, QUAD

Joan Travis, Chair, Derby Hippodrome Restoration Trust

Emeritus Professor Jonathan Powers DL Hon DUniv

Jordan Reynolds, Assistant Editor, The Derby Yearbook

Professor Kathryn Mitchell, Vice-Chancellor, University of Derby

Lucy Bamford, Senior Curator of Art, Derby Museum and Art Gallery

Maggie Tillson, Tourism Promotion Officer, Derby City Council

Matt Edwards, Curator of Visual Art and the Joseph Wright Study Centre, Derby Museums and Art Gallery

Mike Wheeler, Freelance Writer; Adult Education Tutor, WEA

Nicholas Smith, President, former Managing Director, Fourth Generation, and Archivist, John Smith & Sons

Nick Brown, Derby Cathedral Peregrine Project, Derbyshire Wildlife Trust

Paul Elliott, Professor of Modern History, University of Derby

Dr Pete Meakin, Creative Producer, Derby LIVE

Robin Wood, former mayor

Samantha Joanne Luton, Assistant Editor, The Derby Yearbook

Sharon Stevens-Cash, Marketing Director, Derby Festé

Sheena Holland, Designer and Events Organiser, Night Markets

Sian Hoyle, Founder, Derby Book Festival

Sohila Ayman, Assistant Editor, The Derby Yearbook

Soshain Bali, Trustee, Multi-Faith Centre

Stephen Munn, Artistic Director and CEO, Déda

Stoker Devonshire, 12th Duke of Devonshire KCVO CBE DL

Photographers

Alison Loydall

Alistair Hodge (Carnegie)

Bonbon Photography

Richard Tailby

Claire Sutton Images

Gareth Chell

Graham Lucas Commons

Graham Whitmore

Jenny Welch

John Walls Photography

Kev Ryan

Steve Eggleton

Steve Tanner

Stuart Whitehead